Shoulder TO Shoulder

Also by Rodney L. Cooper

Double Bind

THE JOURNEY FROM
ISOLATION TO BROTHERHOOD

Shoulder
TO
Shoulder

RODNEY L. COOPER
PH.D.

ZondervanPublishingHouse
Grand Rapids, Michigan

A Division of HarperCollins*Publishers*

BV
4528.2
.C66
1997

Library of Congress Cataloging-in-Publication Data

Cooper, Rod. 1953– .
    Shoulder to shoulder : the journey from isolation to brotherhood / Rodney L.
Cooper.
        p. cm.
    Includes bibliographical references.
    ISBN: 0-310-21187-5 (hardcover : alk. paper)
    1. Men—Religious life. 2. Men—Conduct of life. 3. Men—Psychology. 4.
Christian life. I. Title.
    BV4528.2.C66 1997
    248.8'42—dc21   97-
1611
                CIP

This edition printed on acid-free paper and meets the American National Standards
Institute Z39.48 standard.

Published in association with the literary agency of Wolgemuth & Hyatt, 8012 Brooks
Chapel Road #243, Brentwood, Tennessee 37027.

Printed in the United States of America

97 98 99 00 01 02 03 04 /❖ DH/ 10 9 8 7 6 5 4 3

Contents

Acknowledgments

There is no question that I would not have been able to experience what I have written about without the following key people:

Nancy Cooper, my wife. No matter how distant I became or depressed I have gotten, Nancy has persistently pursued with Christ's love. She has loved me when I was unlovable. She was gracious to me when I was graceless. Thank you, Honey. I am so glad God has graced my life with you. I am a much better man for it.

Wes Roberts and Harvey Powers. These men are my "Huddle." They believed in me when I didn't. They had faith for me when I couldn't. They have cried, laughed, confronted, and cared. They have literally helped me come out of isolation and into brotherhood. "How sweet and pleasant it is for brothers to dwell in unity" and "there is a friend who sticketh closer than a brother." Thanks—friends.

Bill Perkins. I couldn't have done this book without you, Bill. It was you who helped me break free from my struggles with being black. It was you who said, "I like you, Rod, just because you are Rod." You will never know how that little bit of light brought me out of hiding. Thanks, Buddy.

Glen Wagner and Dan Ireland. We do not see each other a lot, but we are never "out of sight, out of mind." Thanks for being there when I need you and your wise counsel.

Finally, I thank God for my mentors, Haddon Robinson and Howard Hendricks. Thanks, Haddon, for taking me in during those seminary days. Your family became my family. I was only one of three blacks on campus and my dad had just died. You took it upon yourself to care for me during those tough times. You "fathered" me and believed in me. You have always given me wise counsel over the years. Thank you is not adequate—but "THANK YOU."

"Prof" Hendricks, I will never forget what you said when I was struggling with race issues on campus. You said, "Rod, to be black and evangelical, you have to laugh a lot. Because we are so ignorant, and if you do not laugh—you will get angry. Please give us some room—we just do not know." I have laughed a lot. Thank you for putting me in your discipleship group and being there for me over the years. I could have stayed isolated—but you brought me out. I thank God for you, "Prof."

This project would not have been possible were it not for a good brother who helped me "pull it together" along the way. Thanks, Bill. I also want to thank Zondervan Senior Editor Bob Hudson for calling me and encouraging me in the writing of this book. Thanks to Bob and his assistant Robin Schmitt for their wonderful suggestions and helping this book to be truly "readable." Also, thanks to Cheryl for the help on the wonderful discussion questions in the discussion guide. You did good. Finally, thanks to Zondervan for publishing this book. Your support has been exemplary.

Introduction

C. S. Lewis wrote that lovers, facing each other, don't see the world but only each other. Friends, he said, (and it was evident that he considered that the more important relationship) stand together, facing the world and all it throws at them, shoulder to shoulder. In this stance, friends are ready to confront any enemy that comes against them. They share a similar perspective. Hence the title of this book, *Shoulder to Shoulder: The Journey from Isolation to Brotherhood* describes that kind of friendship.

Men feel the pressure today to stand alone. The image of the Hero riding solo into the sunset, leaving friendships and romance behind, is branded in our minds. It shapes how we view ourselves and, unless we make a conscious effort to change, it is how we will shape our sons.

This view is harmful to men physically, mentally and emotionally. Further, this unbiblical view threatens to deaden men spiritually. Jesus gathered a core group of men around him. They ate with him, slept with him, traveled with him. They witnessed his miracles, his laughter, his anger, his love and his tears. In seeing him without a mask, as an authentic man, they saw what they eventually became: transformed men.

But becoming a transformed man, a shoulder to shoulder brother, isn't easy. Many things stand in the way and actually encourage men to remain behind their masks.

Shoulder to Shoulder explores how and why men hide behind masks. It is a book that describes the journey. The first chapter describes hiding, also called the Fig Leaf Phenomenon because Adam was its first player. The next three chapters describe the results of hiding: addiction, stress and a pervading feeling of meaninglessness. The journey doesn't stop there, though. It may be risky to come out of hiding and connect with God and other men. But it's worth it.

The next chapters begin the journey out of hiding with 8 Steps to Building Brotherhood. Each step allows a man to go a little deeper with himself and with God. God, however, doesn't let a man stop there. The Lone Ranger, John Wayne type of Christian doesn't exist in the Bible. There is no riding off into the sunset. God wants us in a community.

I have called this special community "the huddle." As in football, the huddle represents a time of recommitment, a coming together as a team before facing the "enemy." It is a place of safety, rest, trust, direction, encouragement. In short, a place of shoulder-to-shoulder brotherhood.

It isn't easy creating this type of huddle. Society and many of the messages we grew up with encourage just the opposite. That's why I have also written about differing personalities. God created all of us different. And understanding that helps us to better understand our brothers. Accountability is easier when we understand how we and our brothers are wired.

The last chapter talks about the blessings of brotherhood. As I said earlier, the risks are worth it! C. S. Lewis knew the blessings of surrounding himself with a group of men. As you read this book and work through the study questions, remember that the words Robert Browning wrote to his wife can apply to the wonders of being a man in Christ: "Come and grow old with me; the best is yet to be."

PART ONE

—◦—

The Isolated Man

1. Hiding

Adam's first expression of emotion communicated his fear of exposure, which caused him to hide from God. Men work hard to stay hidden, because they fear that if others see what they're really like, they'll be abandoned. This chapter will discuss the ways men hide and the consequences of their secret lives.

2. Addiction

Because men are in isolation, they choose the illusion of intimacy offered through addictive and compulsive behavior. Illicit sex, compulsive work, alcohol, drugs, and other addictions never argue, never fail to give a mood swing, and are always there when needed. This chapter will help the reader understand some of the causes and consequences of compulsive behavior, and the isolation that accompanies it.

3. Stress

The pressure of living in a highly competitive society places men in an adversarial relationship with one another. As a result, men are under constant stress to stay in control of their lives so they can keep a competitive edge. It's hard to open up with other men when they're viewed as the competition. Since men can't depend on others, they feel they have to go it alone. Consequently, men never have an opportunity to let down their guard, and live in a constant state of anxiety.

4. Meaninglessness

Every man wants his life to matter. He wants to feel that he makes a difference. He hopes to leave a legacy to his children. Yet most men aren't sure why they're here. If they achieve their career goals, they often feel unfulfilled and wonder if that's all there is. If they face career roadblocks, they feel like a failure. They fear they'll be seen as a loser. As a result of this, men never hook into life's real meaning and have relationships that help them achieve it.

CHAPTER 1

Hiding

It requires cunning, skill, and quick thinking. You must have a solid strategy and be keenly aware of your surroundings. One mistake or one false move and you are finished. It also requires you to take risks and go places no one else would dream of going. It's quite a game. Interested? I thought so. The name of the game—hide-and-seek.

We've all played hide-and-seek. I'll never forget the first time I played hide-and-seek with my then fiancée, Nancy, and her sister's family. I was visiting Nancy at her parents' house. Nancy wanted me to meet her oldest sister, Susan, and her family. It was about nine in the evening when we arrived at their house in the country. Apparently, we were just in time to play their weekly game of hide-and-seek. I learned that when they play hide-and-seek, it's serious business. First of all, everyone wears black so they'll blend into the darkness. Secondly, all the outside lights are turned off so no one will have an advantage. Finally, no flashlights are allowed, and you can hide anyplace on the premises—but not in the house.

The person doing the seeking has to count to fifty, and then the game's on. The participants in the game were Susan (Nancy's sister), Paul (her brother-in-law), Tabitha (her niece), Eli (her nephew), Nancy, and me.

The first game of hide-and-seek I got caught, because the dog found me and began barking. I could not get him to go away, so I was an easy mark. The other two games I was not found. In fact, the men were usually the best at hiding. I learned that the women tended not to put themselves into dangerous situations, so they would usually pick the safest places to hide. Also, it seemed that they wanted to be found. On the other hand, the guys, for the most part, would put themselves in some pretty dangerous situations. Eli was in a water well, hanging on for dear life, so he would not be found. I was in the rafters in the barn, with the bats. Paul—well—I never did figure out where he was hiding. Suffice it to say that we men would do about anything to stay hidden and not get caught.

I've found that the same is true of men in real life. It seems that we men will do anything to hide and not get caught. There seems to be this incredible, almost instinctual need not to be found out. I've also learned that men play the game very, very well. Women can play the game, but men have made a science and an art out of it. I've counseled hundreds of men and their wives, and the wife raises the same lament over and over again. She usually says, "Why won't he let me into his life? Why won't he share with me? Why can't we have the intimacy that I long to have in this relationship?"

I have to confess that I've found this to be true in my own life. I've been married for fourteen years. I have a wonderful wife who loves me beyond words. But whenever we get close— you know what I mean: a "soul" closeness—I get nervous and scared and want to pull away. It's as if this wall goes up in me, and alarms go off: "Red alert, red alert—Beam me up, Scotty!" By God's grace and the patience of my wife, I've been slowly tearing down the bricks in the wall and have started to come out of hiding—but it has not been easy. We men hide when it comes to deep relationships with others. We have incredible strategies and skills to stay hidden when it comes to experiencing the dynamic, rich, full relationships God wants us to experience with him and with those around us.

Why? Why are we so driven to hide and will do anything and go anywhere to stay hidden? Let us look at the one who started the original game of hide-and-seek and discover the answers.

THE FIG-LEAF PHENOMENON

When the woman saw that the fruit of the tree was good for food and pleasing to the eye, and also desirable for gaining wisdom, she took some and ate it. She also gave some to her husband, who was with her, and he ate it. Then the eyes of both of them were opened, and they realized they were naked; *so they sewed fig leaves together and made coverings for themselves.*

Then the man and his wife heard the sound of the LORD God as he was walking in the garden in the cool of the day, and they *hid* from the LORD God among the trees of the garden. But the LORD God called to the man, "Where are you?"

He answered, "I heard you in the garden, and I was afraid because I was naked; *so I hid.*"

Genesis 3:6–10, emphasis added

Adam was the first one to play the game hide-and-seek. The Lord God wanted to connect with Adam and Eve, but something was terribly wrong. I get the impression from the text that Adam, Eve, and God met regularly about this time— "the cool of the day." I also get the impression that there was no hiding or seeking until now. Apparently, there was great openness and eagerness in getting together until Adam and Eve ate of the forbidden fruit. Yet when they ate—the game was on. This was the first time God had to ask the question, "Where are you?" Notice that the question was directed to the man. Adam was the one directly responsible for keeping the garden in order. He was the one who was to give guidance and protection to Eve. He was the one to answer to God. But he knew he was naked. In other words, he knew he was now unacceptable—shameful. You see, the difference between guilt and shame is that guilt happens as a result of doing wrong, while shame happens because you *are* wrong. For the first time, Adam was wrong—something was broken. Hence the fig-leaf phenomenon. There's the incredible need to cover up this unacceptability. Adam did and so do we men. Every single man suffers from the fig-leaf syndrome. There's not a single man I know who doesn't live with it, doesn't struggle with it, doesn't experience it.

There's a shame that every man feels because he feels wrong. It's not just that he does things wrong but that he actually is wrong on the inside. All because of a profound sense of shame or unacceptability. We attempt to cover ourselves up because we feel unacceptable.

Another reason men attempt to cover up is because of the fear that exposure will lead to abandonment. In other words, if you see me for who I am, you'll judge me and leave me. This is part of the curse that happened to Adam and Eve. They were driven from the garden for their unacceptability, and the result was their feeling abandoned. Part of the curse upon man was that "by the sweat of your brow you will eat your food until you return to the ground, since from it you were taken; for dust you are and to dust you will return" (Gen. 3:19). Part of the curse is an intense feeling of isolation and abandonment. I truly believe that the greatest fear a man has is that he'll be abandoned, especially by those he loves, if they see him for who he really is on the inside. I know it's mine.

I remember coming back from a trip for Promise Keepers. I'd been speaking at one of our conferences. I'd been really scared. I mean, how often do you speak to seventy thousand men in a stadium? I'd also been struggling with the fear that I might fail. I'd desperately wanted to hit the mark in communicating with these men. Yet what would happen, I'd thought, if there was dead silence and I didn't connect? Every speaker I'd heard before me had been tremendous. I'd felt the pressure to perform—to do just as well. I'd realized that this was not the "Great American Preach-Off." I'd known that I was not there to compete but to minister.

Well, I'd given my message and God had blessed the time. Now I was exhilarated, drained, tired, excited, all at the same time. I couldn't wait to tell Nancy about how well it had gone, but that meant also telling her how scared I'd been. When I entered the door, Nancy hugged me and asked me those four key words, "How did it go?" I then responded with my one key word, "Fine." Inside, it seemed a wall had gone up. I, for some irrational reason, felt that if I told Nancy about my fears, I would be judged for not trusting God enough and consequently be abandoned for not being a good spiritual leader. Mind you, Nancy would not have done this, but I still felt that I dare not really share my gut lest I be seen as unacceptable.

Nancy did continue to ask me, and finally I told her about my fear. She only affirmed me and told me how much faith it took to get in front of all those men and be God's spokesman. Nancy didn't abandon me—she blessed me. I truly believe that we men miss tremendous blessings from those around us, due to our belief that if we share our inadequacies, we'll be abandoned. In fact, by being silent, we end up being abandoned, which is the very thing we fear.

You see, we men are to be in control and not be afraid. The popular saying "No fear" is to be our motto. But we *are* afraid. The first emotion of man expressed in the Bible was fear. So what do we do when we are afraid? We hide.

A third reason men are caught in the fig-leaf syndrome is that we must compensate for our feeling of inadequacy. So we work hard to show ourselves as being worthy. We get our righteousness the old-fashioned way—we earn it. In his book *The Silence of Adam,* Larry Crabb writes,

> If a man is honest with himself at the exact moment he feels most threatened, he will admit to feeling terror and self-doubt. At this point, rather than abandoning himself to Christ in humility and faith, and leaving explanations and guarantees behind, he is more likely to ask a self-absorbing question for which there is only one discouraging answer: "Do I have what it takes to handle whatever it is I find threatening?" *He therefore lives in fear, desperately determined to avoid exposure of his inadequacy. He gives little thought to what it would mean to give of himself as a man.*[1]

If these are the reasons men hide, what do men do to cover up their nakedness? How do men hide from themselves, from others, and from God? Let's take a look.

A GOOD DEFENSE IS A GOOD OFFENSE

Men hide emotionally. A man will do just about anything to hide his emotions, especially negative ones such as doubt, shame, guilt, and fear of failure, among others. So a man will erect what we in the counseling business call defense mechanisms. A defense mechanism is a strategy that a person will develop to keep their ego intact and not lose face with those around them. In all my counseling of men, I've discovered that there are four key defense mechanisms that men tend to use to keep the unacceptable part of themselves hidden and to justify their failures. (There are many other defense strategies, but I've discovered that these are the most common.) They are:

1. Rationalization

A man will attempt to prove that his behavior is rational and "justifiable" and thus worthy of self- and social approval. Adam was a master of rationalization. Just listen to his explanation of why he ate of the forbidden fruit: "The man said, 'The woman you put here with me —she gave me some fruit from the tree, and I ate it'" (Gen. 3.12). Imagine Adam saying, "God, this is your fault. I mean, you were the one who thought I needed a companion. I was just naming animals and taking care of the garden, and then the next thing I know, I'm missing a rib and here's this woman in my life. It would only make sense that I would eat of the fruit, since she came from your hand—and I know you wouldn't give me anything or anyone that would harm me."

Men are very adept at minimizing their responsibility and shifting the blame to others. Research has shown that when women fail at a task or make a mistake, their overall tendency is to blame themselves. The same studies show that when men make a mistake or fail at a task, they blame some outside agency. In other words, they didn't get clear instructions or weren't given enough time to complete the job, or the conditions weren't suitable for the task. There's a strong need in men to shift the blame and to maximize the shortcomings of others and minimize their own.

Another great example of this tendency is found in Exodus 32. Let me set the scene. Moses had gone up the mountain to meet with God. Yet before he went, he gave Aaron explicit instructions to keep the people in line and to keep sin out of the camp. Moses had been gone a long time, and the people began to lapse into their customary habit of grumbling. Exodus 32:1 points out that the people wanted to make gods to serve, since

Moses had been gone for such a long time and might not come back. Aaron gives explicit instructions in verse 2 by saying, "Take off the gold earrings that your wives, your sons and your daughters are wearing, and bring them to me." Verse 4 says, "He [Aaron] took what they handed him and made it into an idol cast in the shape of a calf, fashioning it with a tool. Then they said, 'These are your gods, O Israel, who brought you up out of Egypt.'" Aaron was actively involved in this process. He even *made* the calf for the Israelites. Well, Moses did make it back from the mountain and saw what had happened. When he called Aaron to account for his lack of leadership and for leading the people into sin, listen to Aaron's defense:

> "Do not be angry, my lord," Aaron answered. "You know how prone these people are to evil. [Shift the blame.] They said to me, 'Make us gods who will go before us. As for this fellow Moses who brought us up out of Egypt, we don't know what has happened to him.' So I told them, 'Whoever has any gold jewelry, take it off.' Then they gave me the gold, and I threw it into the fire, and out came this calf!"
>
> Exodus 32:22–24

Did you catch the last phrase? "I threw it into the fire, and out came this calf!" Remember, Aaron had delicately carved out the calf in the previous verses. Yet here he just threw the gold into the fire and, gee whiz, out came this calf. I have to laugh. Notice the rationalization, and the maximizing of the children of Israel's part and the minimizing of his own part. Men have a strong tendency to hide behind their rationalizations.

2. Denial of Reality

A man will protect himself from unpleasant reality by his refusal to accept it. In the movie *Good Morning, Vietnam!* radio disc jockey Kronkmeyer, played by Robin Williams, has been

barred from doing his radio show for the troops. There's a lieutenant who believes himself to be incredibly funny and decides
to do the show in Kronkmeyer's place. He bombs—and bombs
badly. In fact, the colonel of the base realizes that this man is
hurting morale among the troops and decides to reinstate
Kronkmeyer. The colonel calls the lieutenant into his office to
inform him of his decision to remove him from the program
because, frankly, he's a lousy comedian. The lieutenant responds,
"Sir, in my heart I know I'm funny." This man will not face reality. He prefers to stay in denial rather than face the painful fact
that he's not very good. I've found this to be true of many men.
Instead of accepting their limitations, they elect to remain in a
state of denial and blame others for their shortcomings.

3. Compensation

A man will cover up a weakness by emphasizing a desirable
trait or making up for frustration in one area by overgratification
in another. In other words, a man will become incredibly competent in one area so his weaknesses in another area will be
ignored. I know of a company in which they have one of the
most successful and hard-driving department managers I've ever
seen. He's incredible with getting the most out of his department and completing projects ahead of schedule and below cost.
The only problem is that his relational skills are deplorable and
he keeps losing people. He has compensated for his lack of
people skills by being an incredible project manager and administrator. Even though he loses people from his department, the
company overlooks his lack of relational skills, because of his
incredible abilities.

4. Emotional Insulation

A man will withdraw into passivity to protect himself from
hurt. I call it stonewalling. I've lost count of the number of
times I've seen this in my counseling of married couples.

His name was Bob and her name was Jill. They had been married for over twenty years and had finally decided to seek counseling. I could see that there were a lot of unresolved issues in this marriage. One in particular was how to handle their finances. Bob made great money as a CPA. Jill also worked, as a nurse. The impasses seemed to come in that Jill perceived that her husband considered the money she made to be "their" money, and the money he made to be "his" money. Jill desperately wanted Bob to concede in this area, but Bob sat passively in the counseling room, saying over and over again one word: "Whatever." No emotion, no passion—just this cold response. I began to hold individual sessions with each of them and learned that Bob had been married before and had felt he could never earn enough to satisfy his first wife's desires. He'd taken on several outside jobs, and instead of being praised for his effort, he was put down. After the divorce he lost just about everything. He decided he would never let this happen again. So he emotionally insulated himself and pulled away from his second wife, especially in this area, because he was determined never to get hurt again.

IT'S WHAT'S ON THE OUTSIDE THAT COUNTS

In the last section we've seen how we men tend to hide ourselves psychologically and emotionally. I call this the internal cover-up. The defense strategies we men use are ways to keep us from facing the fact that we feel shame and will do whatever it takes to cover it up—even lie to ourselves. Yet there are also external fig leaves we use to try to cover ourselves up.

There are two key areas we men will use to hide externally.

One way a man will try to hide is through good deeds and religious activity. He thinks, "As long as I'm doing something for God, maybe I can earn my way back into his good graces and be found acceptable." I've found that many men who are active in the church or who are in the ministry use their position as a cover-up. A friend of mine who is a pastor of a very large church said, "It's amazing to me how many people who are in the ministry use the ministry as simply a fig leaf; who say, 'I'm a good person,' 'I'm an influential person,' 'I'm a special person,' 'I'm somebody who demands respect because of my position or because of my title.'" You see, you can get a fig leaf that has a spiritual color to it. Hiding behind a spiritual title and spiritual activity is one of the most insidious kinds of fig leaves, because it looks so good and feels so good, but it's still not dealing with the reality of who you are as a person. It's simply promoting an image to compensate for feelings of fear, insecurity, inadequacy, shame, and even embarrassment.

There are men who are Sunday school teachers, deacons, on the board of elders, and very active in the church but are using these positions and the good works they do to cover up the incredible sense of unacceptability they feel toward God, others, and themselves.

There's a passage of Scripture that has always haunted me. It says, "Not everyone who says to me, 'Lord, Lord,' will enter the kingdom of heaven, but only he who does the will of my Father who is in heaven. Many will say to me on that day, 'Lord, Lord, did we not prophesy in your name, and in your name drive out demons and perform many miracles?' Then I will tell them plainly, 'I never knew you. Away from me, you evildoers!'" (Matt. 7:21–23).

There are two key points that impress me from this passage. First of all, God is more interested in authenticity than he is in activity. The motives for many of these people doing ministry—which, by the way seemed to be very public, such as preaching, driving out demons, and performing miracles—were personal satisfaction and public approval.

Secondly, "doing the will of the Father" requires total surrender of my agenda and complete submission to his. In other words, I cannot hide, and I must be completely openhanded with God so I can do his will. Corrie ten Boom put it well when she said, "I have learned not to hold on to anything too tightly because it hurts too much to have God pry back my fingers to get to it. So I have learned to live my life with an open hand. That way God can put in and take out whatever he wants and I never miss the blessing."

Yet I've found that all too often we can substitute religious activity as a way to compensate for our feelings of unacceptability. I work for the fastest-growing Christian organization to date—Promise Keepers. It's very easy to get caught up in ministering to literally thousands of men, hopefully impacting families and marriages for the good. But I also know that there's a tendency to rely on these "good works" rather than doing the hard work of being openly accountable to a friend when I've looked at the previews of an adult movie or lusted after another woman in my heart. It's only when I'm authentic—when the secrets are out—that I can truly be cleansed by God and then be of service to God.

A second way we men try to hide externally is through social standing. When I think of social standing, I think of the four P's. They are: performance, position, power, and possessions. In other words, if I *perform* with excellence and better than anyone else, I can reach the right *position* in my job or career, which will give me the *power* (power being defined as doing what I want when I want) to accumulate the *possessions* required to show success and acceptability. The only problem with this formula is that it's completely dependent on my performance. So what happens when somebody comes along who can perform better than me? You got it—there goes my security and significance.

I remember holding chapel for the Pittsburgh Steelers when they were in their glory years. I'm talking about Terry

Bradshaw, Franco Harris, Donnie Shell, John Stallworth, Lynn Swann, Mike Webster, Mel Blount, and the list goes on and on. Most of the guys I mentioned above came to the chapel service. I talked on the subject "Is there life after football?" I pointed out that over fifty percent of the men in chapel that day would not be there the next year because somebody better would come along or they would be injured and could no longer play. I asked the question, "If you were to sustain a career-ending injury today—would it affect your identity? Where do you ultimately place your trust?" I explained that when they trusted Christ, there was a no-cut clause. He would always care for them and love them no matter what.

After the message, Franco Harris came up to me and said, "You know, I'd love to *know* I was accepted no matter what. You see, even though I'm at the top of my game, I have no assurance that enough is enough. I've been with the team so long that I just figured that I'd be there next year. I thought I was secure. But I'm learning that there are no guarantees. There's this little voice always in the back of my mind saying, 'Have you done enough?'" The next year Franco Harris was cut.

I believe Franco summed up the two key consequences that happen when a man hides or attempts to cover himself up with fig leaves. First of all, he develops a superficial sense of security. For a while he feels pretty good about himself. But secondly, he knows that he's always in competition and could at any time be uncovered. Therefore he has this nagging sense that he might not be covered enough. I believe that many men can relate to the saying I saw on a painting of a lion with a gazelle in the background. The saying goes like this: "Every morning a lion and a gazelle wake up in Africa. The gazelle knows that if it's going to survive, it must be able to run faster than the fastest lion. The lion knows that if he's going to eat that day, he must be able to run faster than the slowest gazelle. When they wake up . . . they wake up running."[2]

So do many men. No matter how well they feel they have hidden themselves, they wake up running to stay hidden. But eventually they are caught and uncovered—and when they are, the effects can be devastating.

For twenty-five years he'd lived a Thoreau-like existence in a crude shack five miles from Lincoln, Montana. He was an intensely private man—polite but aloof. He was known as a bearded eccentric who would pedal his bicycle into town to get supplies and then return to his shack. Little did anyone realize that this man was incredibly brilliant. He'd graduated from high school two years early, at age sixteen had gone to Harvard University on a math scholarship, and had ended up getting a Ph.D. in math from the University of Michigan. He went on to teach at the University of California at Berkeley. It seemed he showed all the promise of being a brilliant professor with a long career in academia. But suddenly he felt the need to quit his position and go, oddly enough, into hiding. Who would've thought that a man with such a brilliant mind would end up in a shack in Montana, barely eking out his existence through odd jobs?

But that's exactly what Theodore Kaczynski did. He went into hiding because he could not cope with the incredible demands of life. Yet he also resented those who seemed to be putting the pressure on him. "Those" happened to be society at large. He would periodically come out of hiding long enough to show his displeasure with society; then he would go back into hiding. But finally he was uncovered. Ted Kaczynski was an angry man. You see, that's what happens when you go into hiding. You get mad because you feel misunderstood, so you end up lashing out at those around you, because of the incredible feeling of unacceptability. We may not, as Ted Kaczynski has allegedly done, resort to mailing pipe bombs to people to show our anger. But what we do has the potential to explode in our faces and in the lives of those we love.

Hiding can have dangerous results, because it creates incredible distortions and removes us from dealing with reality. In the next three chapters, we'll discover and describe three key consequences of staying hidden.

DISCUSSION QUESTIONS

1. Read Genesis 3:6–10. Why did God ask Adam where he was?
2. Discuss the difference between shame and guilt? Why did Adam and Eve feel shame?
3. Dr. Cooper wrote that "the greatest fear a man has is that he will be _____." Do you agree or disagree? Give your reasons. Has there been a time you felt you missed a blessing due to this fear?
4. Dr. Cooper wrote that men would rather stay in denial than face a painful reality. Read John 18:28. How did the priests deny reality? What would have happened if they had corporately faced reality?
5. As a group watch the movie *City Slickers*. Discuss Ed's character and how he compensates to cover up a weakness or a fear.
6. "It is only when I am authentic—when the secrets are out—that I can truly be cleansed by God and then be of service for God." Read 2 Samual 11:1–12:23 and Psalm 51. How did David finally become authentic? How was David authentic with God? With Nathan? With Bathsheba?
7. How do you use spiritual activity to promote an image? Is this image consistent with reality?

CHAPTER 2

Addiction

It was one of those days. I mean, it was the kind of day in which driving down the freeway behind a group of Hell's Angels and having my horn get stuck would have been an improvement. Yep, it was one of those days.

Feeling down, I decided to do something that would make me feel better. I made up my mind that I'd give myself a treat at one of my favorite hangouts—a trendy men's clothing store. It was just what I needed.

As I ran my fingers over the new shirts, I found a couple that were just right. Of course, I needed some slacks to go with them. "Not a problem," the salesman assured me. In no time I'd selected two new shirts and a couple pairs of pants.

The only problem I saw was the price on the sales slip—those clothes weren't cheap. In fact, they definitely fit into the "expensive" category. I walked out of the store feeling better and worse. The clothes looked great, but I'd put myself in a financial bind by charging them. I also hesitated in telling Nancy, because I knew she wouldn't be too happy about what I'd done.

Later that evening I showed her the latest additions to my wardrobe. She praised my selection and then asked the question

I'd hoped to avoid: "Rod, why did you buy those clothes when you've already spent your clothing budget?"

Her question really irritated me. So what if I'd spent more than we had budgeted? It wasn't as if I were running up anything like the federal deficit.

I kept the clothes and even wore one of the combinations to work the next day. And I got the rave reviews I'd looked forward to. In fact, I'm known for my dapper wardrobe. The product people at Promise Keepers even consult me about their latest choices on shirts and pants.

As you've guessed by now, I have a problem in this area. I love clothes. And I love the experience of buying them. I've often wondered why. I think it may stem back to my days in junior high school, when I was overweight and couldn't wear anything. I lost a lot of weight when I entered senior high school, and began to buy clothes to show off my manly body. The "Oohs!" and "Aahs!" felt good. And they still do.

And now, years later, I still buy clothes because it makes me feel good when people turn their head and admire my wardrobe. I hate to admit it, but this craving for clothes and the affirmation they bring smacks of an addiction.

It's not that buying clothes or looking good is an addiction. They're not. But I buy them for a mood change. I nurture myself in this way. And it's not all that easy for me to keep it under control. The problem is, if I don't bridle this area of compulsion, it can do serious damage to my life. It can undermine my ministry and marriage and consequently keep me out of relationships. It can keep me in hiding.

WHEN ARE WE HOOKED?

Most of us have something we turn to when we're down. Something that gives us a mood swing. Something that makes us feel better fast. The problem is, if we go back to that "something" often enough, we get to where we can't resist its lure. And once we're hooked, it demands our heart and soul. It threatens to destroy us. That's why it's so important for us to understand our compulsive behavior and know how to restrain it.

But when are we really hooked? At what point does a craving for something become an addiction? To answer that question, we need to understand what an addiction is.

- Dr. Gerald G. May, author of *Addiction and Grace,* defines an addiction as "any compulsive, habitual behavior that limits the freedom of human desire. It is caused by the attachment, or nailing, of human desire to specific objects."[1]
- In his book *The Pleasure Addicts,* Lawrence Hatterer wrote that a person can be considered addicted when an "overpowering, repetitive, excessive need exists for some substance, object, feeling, act, milieu, or personal interaction."[2]
- In *The Addictive Personality,* Dr. Craig Nakken states, "Addiction is a pathological love and trust relationship with an object or event."[3]

Those definitions, all of which are helpful, come from men who have worked with countless addicts. I've gleaned some less-professional definitions from a few men I've counseled.

- "Addiction," said one man, "is an appetite that begs to be fed. It won't stop pleading until I satisfy it. And then it's only silent for a while."
- Another man said, "It's something that's on my mind almost all the time. If I'm awake, I'm either feeling guilty about what I've done, thinking about doing what I shouldn't, or doing it."

- A former addict said, "It's a terrible thing. I know if I even think about giving in, I'm sunk."

There are almost as many definitions of addiction as there are experiences they represent. So, you may wonder, which one's right? Actually, they all are. Some describe the cause, some the effects, some the condition, some the symptoms, and some the pain.

My favorite definition is the one articulated by my friend Bill Perkins. He defines an addict as "a person who is unable to resist the repeated urge to enter into a love relationship with an object or event for the pleasure and illusion of intimacy it provides."[4]

That definition has three parts:

1. When we're hooked on something, we can't say no.
2. The object of our compulsion gives us great pleasure.
3. The process or substance to which we're addicted gives us the illusion of intimacy. This is a crucial element, one every man needs to realize. Addictions are an enemy of real intimacy and prevent us from developing close relationships.

When we're hooked, our entire lives are centered around pursuing the object or event with which we've developed a love relationship. Often we're not even consciously aware we've become hooked. In a very real sense, our addictions are both secret and hidden—even from us.

In the early stages we aren't even aware a problem exists. We reason that glancing at an erotic magazine once in a while isn't a big deal. Neither is a little playful flirting. Nor is an occasional drink, an extra snack, or buying one more toy we don't really need.

Once we realize—or someone helps us realize—that we can't control our cravings, the addiction is no longer hidden from us. We're aware a problem exists. Yet we try to keep our addiction a secret. We're embarrassed to admit that something, anything, has hooked us. In fact, we may keep it a secret so long, we convince ourselves it's not really an addiction. That's what I did when it came to my clothes problem. I was terribly embarrassed that something as simple as not buying clothes seemed to be beyond my control. I felt ashamed.

If you're like me, you probably wonder how something so obviously harmful could get its hooks in your skin. While nobody can identify a single cause of an addiction, the process of addiction follows a well-worn path. Indeed, by returning to the Garden of Eden, we can see the emergence of a pattern. While Adam and Eve weren't addicted to the forbidden fruit, I want to return to their story because it illustrates what happens to people in the early stages of an addiction. And it shows how some of the defense mechanisms I mentioned in the last chapter not only enable us to hide from others but enable us to carry out behavior that hurts and further isolates us.

SELF-DECEPTION

Eve's problem escalated when she convinced herself the forbidden fruit would give her wisdom. Granted, Satan had planted the lie in her mind. But the more Eve thought about it, the more sense the lie made to her. She must have reasoned, "Could something that looks so good really be all that bad?"

Sounds familiar, doesn't it?

Later she concluded, "If I eat the fruit, it'll give me life!" What a trap she stepped into. And what a lie she believed.

Unfortunately, we sometimes fail to learn from her example. We see the trap and still step into it, thinking its teeth won't snap shut and grab us. But they do. And the moment we realize we're caught by an addiction and can't get loose, we develop a system of faulty reasoning that justifies our actions. We have to. Otherwise we couldn't live with ourselves.

One man I counseled several years ago said he'd learned to beat the system in the hotels where he stayed during business trips. The pay television allowed five free preview minutes. He discovered that five minutes gave him all the time he needed with his favorite erotic flicks.

As we talked, he revealed a sophisticated system of self-deception. "Hey," he said, "it's not like I'm paying for it. Besides, I'm not watching the entire movie. I can honestly tell my wife and friends that I've never seen or rented a porno flick."

Since he felt buying an X-rated movie would be wrong, as would watching an entire pornographic film, he convinced himself his behavior was OK. After all, he *never* paid for a minute of it.

In the early stages of an addiction, we believe such lies. We don't realize we're distorting reality to justify our behavior. Our explanation makes perfect sense. My client convinced himself it was OK to watch pornographic movie scenes, since he wasn't paying to watch an entire film.

Such thinking reminds me of a *Far Side* cartoon in which a dog is pictured leaning out the passenger window of a car, taunting a neighbor dog. As the car backs out of the driveway, the dog said, "Naa, naa, naa, naa, naa. I'm going to the vet to get *tutored*."

The dog's reasoning made sense, but it wasn't linked to reality. Since the dog thought he was going to get tutored, he was excited about the car ride.

In a sense, that's the kind of thinking that characterizes addicts. They redefine reality to justify their behavior. Unfortunately, they believe that their distortion of reality is accurate. And since they've deceived themselves, they see no reason to change. Like Eve, they not only eat the fruit, they offer it to others.

FINGER POINTING

As I noted in the last chapter, we men are experts at shifting responsibility away from ourselves and onto someone, or something, else. That's why it's no surprise that when God asked Adam if he'd disobeyed, Adam pointed a finger at Eve and said, "It's her fault" (Gen. 3:11–12). Adam didn't want to face the truth about what he'd done. He hoped to minimize the seriousness of his sin by blaming his wife. Like Adam, addicts deceive themselves by denying the seriousness of their problem and blaming others.

I've counseled alcoholics who said, "I'm not an alcoholic. I'm a social drinker." Of course, they choose to "social drink" several hours a night. Gamblers will declare, "I'm not an addict. Golfers spend far more on their recreation than I do." Sex addicts will tell me, concerning their compulsive masturbation and use of pornography, "It's not like I'm having sex with another person." I've had men tell me such behavior actually strengthens their marriage.

I've become an expert at denying the seriousness of my buying compulsion. A while back I realized my desire for nice watches was a real problem. I just had to get certain types of watches, such as a Seiko Chronograph or a Swiss army watch. I wanted a watch I thought would impress others. Yet I would go into mini-debt to get one. Did you catch what I said? I called the consequences of my spending money on watches *mini*-debt. By identifying my debt as "mini," I was denying the seriousness of my problem.

Few men in the early stages of an addiction will admit they're hooked and need help. Instead, they deceive themselves into believing that their behavior is acceptable.

RATIONALIZATIONS

I noted earlier that men use rationalization to justify their behavior. Now I want to show how it sets up a man for addictive behavior if it's not dealt with.

First, I need to mention that there's a difference between denial and rationalization. When we deny something, we refuse to admit it. When we rationalize something, we give good *reasons* for our behavior instead of admitting the one true reason.[5] Rationalization enables us to distract ourselves and others from the true nature of our problem.

For instance, an alcoholic may say he drinks at night because it helps him fall asleep. A shopping addict will say he spends a fortune on clothes because it's important to his career. A sex addict may insist he reads pornography because his mate doesn't meet his sexual needs. Workaholics might reason that if they didn't work such long hours, the job wouldn't get done.

All these reasons sound legitimate, but they don't address the real problem. One man I know of managed to break free from a twenty-year alcohol addiction. A short time later he got hooked on pain medication. When a friend tried to help him realize the seriousness of his problem, he said, "I'm not addicted to these pills. I need them for my pain."

Even though every member of his family knew the man suffered from an addiction, he rationalized away his problem. From his perspective, he wasn't addicted; he was merely relieving his pain. As long as he could rationalize his need for those pills, he would never have to change his addictive behavior.

ISOLATION

Nothing characterizes the early stages of an addiction more than withdrawal. Slowly, over time, addicts pull away from God and other people. They increasingly turn to the object of their addiction.

If you're like me, you probably wonder why. The reason may surprise you. Addicts seek isolation because the process, person, or substance to which they're addicted gives them an illusion of intimacy. And they have to make a choice between their addiction and other relationships. They can't have it both ways. It's impossible for them to draw close to something they're addicted to and also draw near to God and other people. There's no way it can be done. Jesus said as much when he declared, "No one can serve two masters. Either he will hate the one and love the other, or he will be devoted to the one and despise the other" (Matt. 6:24).

True intimacy is addiction's greatest enemy. Since our addictions give us an illusion of intimacy, only the real thing can burst the bubble of that illusion. Yet as the addiction progresses, we fear telling anyone about it. We're afraid they'll reject and abandon us. Besides, we men like to think we can handle it by ourselves. So instead of reaching out to God and other people, we withdraw and isolate ourselves.

THE ADDICTIVE CYCLE

So far in this chapter, I've described the defense mechanisms that can lead to addictive behavior. Now I'd like to walk you through the addictive cycle. The addictive cycle is a four-step process we go through every time we act out compulsively.

Preoccupation

In most instances, the addictive cycle is triggered by feelings of despair, discouragement, or boredom. When we feel low, we want a mood swing. And so we begin to think about something that'll make us feel better. When we're preoccupied with something, we think about it. In fact, we think about it all the time. As kids, most of us remember becoming preoccupied with wanting a bike or a train set for Christmas. It was all we could think about. And it was all we could talk to our parents about.

The reason this stage is so dangerous is because it's so seemingly innocent. After all, what harm is there in *thinking* about sex, food, or alcohol? Initially our thoughts may be innocent. But the more we think about it, the more our craving for the object of our thoughts grows. Before long our thoughts begin to sound like the Toyota commercial that said, "You *need* a Toyota!"

Yes, we're good at convincing ourselves that something we *want* is something we *need*. I know, because I've been down that route with watches, shoes, and sweaters. Other men find themselves daydreaming about nachos, beer, and salsa. Many men fantasize about blondes, brunettes, and redheads.

Of course, Jesus realized the power of our thoughts. That's why he told the religious hypocrites of his day, "You have minds like a snake pit! How do you suppose what you say is worth anything when you are so foul-minded? It's your heart, not a dictionary, that gives meaning to your words."[6]

Our thoughts are powerful because our speech and actions flow from them. Of course, we don't usually leap from a sinful thought to a sinful act. Instead, we take a series of small, seemingly harmless steps, or rituals.

Ritualization

Because the rituals appear innocent, we can participate in them with little internal resistance. In *Sane Society*, Erich Fromm states that in a ritual, a person "acts out with his body what he thinks out with his brain."[7]

I can tell you, I'm well acquainted with rituals. As an avid golf fan, I enjoy not only playing the game but watching it on TV. And like the rest of America, I'm pretty impressed with Tiger Woods. Of course, like everyone else on the pro tour, he's a sharp dresser. And while watching him one Sunday afternoon, I couldn't help but notice the sharp sweater he was wearing. It was the latest style and made me realize I was a bit behind the times with my sweater wardrobe.

Of course, such thinking is no big deal. But I went from the thought to the morning paper, where I began to scan the pages for clothing sales. In that moment I moved from preoccupation to ritualization. My next ritual would be to browse the aisles of a men's clothing store—with no intention to buy. Honest! I was just looking. That's all. Nothing more.

For a man with a sexual compulsion, rituals might include channel surfing, driving through a red-light district, or examining the labels on some sexually explicit videos. A food addict might shop on an empty stomach. An alcoholic might drop by his favorite bar just to visit with some friends.

We ritualize the actions we find exciting. Before long we can experience exhilaration by just thinking about a ritual. This experience serves a crucial role. It provides a rush of excitement and prepares us for the next step.

Acting Out

Once we've begun to ritualize, it's inevitable that we'll act out. The two are linked by an unbroken chain. While the rituals may last for days or weeks, acting out always follows.

James, the half-brother of Jesus, described the process. He said, "Each one is tempted when, by his own evil desire, he is dragged away and enticed. Then, after desire has conceived, it gives birth to sin; and sin, when it is full-grown, gives birth to death" (James 1:14–15).

Note the cycle: enticement (preoccupation), conception (ritualization), birth (acting out), death (shame). As certain as birth follows conception, so acting out follows ritualization.

Shame

It's tragic that something that promises so much delivers so little. Something we felt we couldn't live without creates nothing but shame—a deep sense that we aren't right. And with the shame comes a more intense drive to withdraw further from God and those we love.

Addiction can be like an octopus—once it wraps its tentacles around you, it can smother the very life out of you. It'll take you places you never thought you would go, and in the end you'll be devastated. Just ask Samson. He was a he-man—with a she-problem.

The moment he was introduced into the biblical record, so was his problem. Samson told his parents he'd seen a Philistine woman and wanted them to get her for him (Judg. 14:1–3). Samson wanted a non-Jewish woman. One who was off-limits. Well, he got her—and all the problems that came with her.

After her premature death, Samson seemed to have his problem under control. And then as he approached the middle of his life, the beast broke loose from its harness. Again Samson went looking for a Philistine woman, and he found Delilah. The details of their sordid affair are the stuff movies are made of (literally). Ultimately Samson lost his hair, his position, his eyes, and his honor. All because he couldn't say no to a compulsive appetite for sexual pleasure that was off-limits.

He discovered too late that when the cycle is repeated, the addiction becomes more intense and unbreakable. Eventually the addict raises the white flag. He gives up. When that happens, a man is totally isolated from God and other people.

A SAFETY NET

Later I'll talk more extensively about how a man can find lasting freedom from his compulsions. But I want to mention now that the key is connecting with God and another man or men. Why? Because the illusion of intimacy can only be overcome by real intimacy. Nothing else works.

A number of years ago I remember reading the story of one of the world's greatest tightrope walkers. For decades this man, with nothing but a long pole in his hands, had fearlessly walked on a cable between skyscrapers, hundreds of feet above the ground. But one day while his family and hundreds of spectators watched, he tried a daring walk on a windy day. All alone, far above the street below, he lost his balance. Because the cable was swaying, he couldn't regain his footing. As a world-renowned tightrope walker, he never allowed a safety net below the cable. So when he fell—he plummeted to his death.

How tragic. But just as tragic is the man who tries to make it through life without a safety net—without a friend to catch him if he should slip. When we choose to hide from others, we run the risk of falling into an addiction.

There's another danger that's just as great. Let's look at it in the next chapter.

DISCUSSION QUESTIONS

1. What do you turn to for a mood swing?
2. Addictions are the enemy of real _____ and prevent us from developing close relationships.
3. What deceptions do you tell yourself in order to deny reality? How do you minimize? Rationalize?
4. If you are not an addict, what areas for you bear watching and accountability?
5. Dr. Cooper states that the only thing that can destroy an addiction's illusion of intimacy is the real thing. Do you have at least one person to whom you can reach out? If not, what steps can you take now to get there?
6. _____ is the first step in the addiction cycle. Read Philippians 4:8 and discuss how this can derail the cycle.
7. Can you identify your rituals?

Chapter 3

Stress

One day I saw a cartoon that consisted of a single picture. In the middle of the frame was a large blender filled with water and a single fish. With a wide-eyed, panicked look, the fish says, "I can't stand it!"

Talk about stress. That poor fish lives with the constant reality that at any minute he could be ripped into a thousand pieces. I think what makes that cartoon so striking is that a lot of men feel the same way. We're surrounded by so many pressures that on almost any day, we feel we could be ripped apart financially, emotionally, relationally, or physically. And the toll of living under such constant pressure is high. Very high!

As you read these words, you may be feeling a bit like that fish yourself. In fact, one of the severe consequences of hiding is being stressed out because of our self-imposed isolation. We'll talk more about that later in the chapter. We'll also look at the damaging consequences of stress. But first I want to provide you with a definition of stress.

Stress is the response of the sympathetic nervous system to a perceived or actual threat. I realize that this technical definition probably won't mean much to you. Basically it says that stress is the way our body responds to perceived or actual danger. Our blood pressure skyrockets and our muscle strength increases. We're ready to fight or fly. Stress isn't a cause but an effect. It's not an action but a reaction.[1]

When we're actually in a dangerous situation, stress is helpful. In fact, it can save our lives. I heard about a hiker who was trekking across the Rocky Mountains when he saw a grizzly bear heading down the trail, straight for him. Instantly his body went into stress. As his heart pounded, it pumped adrenaline throughout his body. Amazingly the man managed to escape. Later when a friend asked him how he got away, he said he grabbed a tree branch that was twenty feet off the ground. "How did you manage that?" his friend asked.

The hiker replied, "I jumped as high as I could and grabbed it on my way down."

While that story is an exaggeration, it illustrates how stress can give a man superhuman strength. It can enable us to run faster and fight harder than we ever imagined possible. Stress prepares our bodies to meet the immediate physical demands of a given situation.

All that's the good news. The bad news is that most men experience stress when there's no real danger. Stress is intended to help save our lives. It's good. But when I get stressed out because of the demands I face at work, I'm not facing an immediate physical threat. Yet I've programmed my mind to perceive it as a threat. The result? My body responds exactly as it would if I were cornered by a mountain lion. My heart rate increases, as does my blood pressure. My muscles tense up and I'm prepared to fight, just like a warrior. But my enemy isn't a mountain lion—it's a six-inch-thick "do list."

I remember an episode of *Star Trek* in which Spock and Captain Kirk found themselves in what appeared to be a life-threatening situation. Surrounded by enemies, they had no choice but to fight. Eventually they realized they were in a no-win situation. Why? Because an alien civilization had created a lifelike illusion. There were no enemies at all—only the enemies of their imagination. Yet Spock and Captain Kirk were fighting as though they faced a *real* danger.

THE HIGH PRICE OF STRESS

When we stress out over an imaginary threat, the consequences are severe. For a short time, in the face of real danger, our minds and bodies can handle and work through stress. But over time it's destructive. Imagine two children on a seesaw. They represent life without stress, in which balance is easily maintained. Now imagine two elephants on the same seesaw. They represent life under stress. If you try to balance a seesaw with two elephants instead of two kids, all sorts of problems emerge.

To begin with, the potential energy of the two elephants is wasted trying to balance on the seesaw. They could be mowing the yard (imagine that) or painting the house (hopefully, without a ladder). We waste energy when we divert energy from long-term, priority projects to solve short-term, stress-inducing emergencies.

Another problem occurs because the elephants do a lot of damage—they smash flowers while entering the playground, not to mention the mammoth droppings they leave all over the lawn. The seesaw wears out much faster when they try to balance themselves on it. The same thing happens to us when we're under stress—we do more harm than good to those around us, and our bodies break down faster.

Finally, if the elephants ever do get balanced on the seesaw, it's hard to get them off. If one hops off, the other will come crashing to the ground. Similarly, when men train themselves to respond in a stressful way to all sorts of life situations, they often find they can't get off the stressful seesaw.[2]

Of course, we know that elephants would never try their luck on a seesaw—I don't think I've ever seen that act at a circus. But we men do face stressful situations that inflict a lot of damage. And it's not just to grass and flowers. Consider some of the destructive consequences of uncontrolled stress.

> *Hypertension.* When doctors talk about hypertension, they're referring to chronic, or consistent, high blood pressure. Blood pressure rises, sending more blood through the arteries, if the heart rate increases or if the vessels constrict (get narrower). Over the short haul this can be good. But it's deadly over the long haul. Why? Because for the heart to supply blood through constricted arteries, the heart has to work harder than God designed it to work. The additional work can cause the heart to enlarge, while its own supply of blood remains the same. That means the heart will be doing more work with fewer nutrients. The result can be painful spasms or heart failure.
>
> The increased blood pressure can burst an artery or push a blood clot into a smaller vessel. If the brain's affected, we call it a stroke. If the heart's damaged, we refer to it as a heart attack.[3]

> *Atherosclerosis.* This is the process by which fatty deposits build up on the inner lining of the arteries. As the arteries are coated with these deposits, they become less elastic and less able to flex when blood is pumped through them. A large part of the waxy, fatty substance that can coat the artery walls is cholesterol. While cholesterol is brought into our bodies when we eat such things as eggs and bacon, most of it is produced by the liver. Under stress, not only does blood pressure go up but so may the amount of cholesterol in the blood.

As blood flow dwindles and cholesterol climbs, a man's anxiety about his health is added to the stresses that helped produce the condition in the first place.[4]

Ulcers. These are usually thought of as being more painful than life-threatening. Yet almost six thousand deaths occur every year in our country due to ulcers, most of them in men. And in most instances, stress is directly linked to the development of an ulcer. Amazingly, they can begin in men who are in their early twenties.[5]

Alcoholism While alcohol doesn't really work to relieve stress, it can temporarily deaden the pain. However, when a man sobers up, he feels worse than before he got drunk. Alcohol actually exaggerates a bad mood. And its abuse creates relational problems that only make the stressful circumstances worse.[6]

Sexual Dysfunction. When the body undergoes stress, it has a dramatic effect on a man's reproductive system. With the onset of stress, testosterone concentrations plunge. In a celebrated study several decades ago, military psychiatrists measured the hormone levels of officer candidate school trainees who had endured an enormous amount of physical and psychological stress. Amazingly, testosterone levels were down. Stress doesn't just affect a man's heart and stomach, it affects his reproductive system.

Two other related problems associated with stress are impotency (inability to get an erection) and premature ejaculation. A number of studies have shown that in more than half the males visiting their doctor to complain of reproductive dysfunction, the problem turned out to be due to stress rather than disease.[7]

Obviously, to a man a problem with sexual performance is more disruptive than a problem with testosterone and sperm production. Most men aren't too concerned about their testosterone levels, but if they can't perform sexually, that's a major issue for most guys.

I've pointed out the severe consequences of stress because I think it's important for you to understand that we're not talking about a small problem here. Like an acid, stress can eat away at your mental and physical well-being. It can literally kill you. Maybe after reading about the dangers of stress, you're wondering if the stress you're experiencing is affecting you. To find out, check yourself on the summary of general stress symptoms below.

_____irritable bowel syndrome

_____swallowing problems

_____hyperventilation

_____asthma

_____rheumatoid arthritis

_____allergies

_____skin disorders

_____heartburn

_____cold sweats

_____anxiety attacks

_____constipation or diarrhea

_____chest pains

_____dizziness

_____chronic fatigue

_____headaches

_____insomnia

_____high blood pressure

_____high cholesterol

_____heart attack

_____peptic ulcer
_____alcoholism
_____erectile dysfunction
_____premature ejaculation

If you have even one check on this list, stress is probably involved. Even the disorders on the list that aren't caused by stress can be aggravated by it.[8]

WHY IS LIFE SO STRESSFUL?

Realizing that stress is a serious problem with severe consequences is the first step we need to take. The second is understanding why so many men suffer from stress.

In his excellent book *Angry Men, Passive Men,* Marvin Allen said he tells men in his groups, "It's as if society requires them to live in a box labeled MAN. Scrawled on the outside of the MAN BOX are dozens of rules: 'Compete.' 'Succeed.' 'Perform.' 'Don't feel.' 'Don't reveal any weakness.' 'Get a grip.' 'Tough it out.' 'Ignore your physical symptoms.' 'Win at all costs.' 'Have all the answers.' 'Fix all the problems.'"[9]

While some of the man-box expectations may work to our advantage, they also create expectations that we feel obligated to meet. And if we can't—or feel that we can't—meet them, our identity as a man may be threatened. How do we respond to such a perception of danger? All too often we stress out. Since that's the case, let's look a bit more closely at the man box.

The Isolated Man

If three words describe how men are supposed to handle life, those words are, "Do it alone!" As we saw in chapter 1, men like to play hide-and-seek. We don't want others to see what's taking place on the inside. If we're open about our needs, others might see us as vulnerable. And no man who is vulnerable would be seen as a formidable adversary. If there's one thing men want to be, it's formidable. At a recent weekend men's retreat, a friend of mine said that the first thought on a man's mind when he enters a room full of men is, "I can take him. I can take him. I'm not so sure I can take him." He was just kidding, but he wasn't far from the truth. A man wants to know he can stand on his own.

When does this isolation begin? It starts as soon as we can understand speech.

Building the Box at Home

Shortly after birth the training of a boy begins. And what are the messages we receive while growing up? Even in supportive homes, boys may be told such things as:

"Big boys don't cry!"
"You don't have anything to cry about."
"That didn't hurt."

Man, whenever I hear that last line, I can't help but remember how bad some of my childhood experiences did hurt. Falling off a bike isn't a picnic. Neither is tripping over a rake and skinning your knee. I can remember being told, "It doesn't hurt *that* bad," and thinking, "Oh yeah, well it sure feels to me like it hurts that bad."

We're told other things, like:

"Tough it out."
"If you don't stop crying, I'll give you something to cry about."
"Stop being a sissy."

Of course, not every boy is subjected to such cutting remarks. Some parents just urge their son to "act like a man." And what does that mean? It means stuffing your feelings inside and refusing to express them. It means not allowing someone else to help you. It means stepping inside the man box and making it on your own.

Adding to the Box As Adults

It would be great if as we matured, we realized we were living in this box. But we don't. Instead, we actually put the finishing touches on it. How? By learning to play hurt on the playing field. By ignoring physical pain in our daily lives. By believing that we men can't be sick because we have to work, work, work. We not only deny our emotions, we deny the symptoms of illness as well.

To that we add:

"I have to achieve."
"I have to be on time."
"I have to hold up my end."
"I have to be a devoted father and husband."
"I have to be a committed Christian."

While there's nothing inherently wrong with any of these, they can become harmful when they define who we are. Over time a man may lose touch with who he really is. Instead, he walks around inside the man box, doing all he can to make others believe he lives up to the words on the side of the box. Anytime he feels he doesn't measure up, a man's identity is threatened. And stress is the natural response to that perceived threat.

Summing It Up

In a sense, we've bought into an artificial label of who we are as men. And then we work hard at convincing ourselves and others that we fit the label. Any perceived shortcoming is responded to with stress. The problem of stress is compounded by our unwillingness to reveal our fears, doubts, and shortcomings to others—especially other men.

MANAGING YOUR STRESS

Two things are at the core of stress: a distorted identity and misplaced faith. We've labeled that distorted identity the man box. The misplaced faith occurs when a man trusts in himself rather than God to meet his most basic needs. Breaking out of the box involves gaining a new identity and transferring our faith to God.

Of course, stress isn't new. Men struggled with the problem in the Lord's day just as they do today. One thing that's impressive about Jesus is that he didn't hesitate to tackle a tough problem. When he saw his followers stressed out by financial concerns, he told them to stop worrying. But he did more than that—he told them why they shouldn't worry. And then he gave them an antidote to help relieve their stress.

The True You

In terms of their identity, Jesus made it clear they were God's children. Because most of us have heard that so many times, it may have become trite. But being a child of God addresses the issue of your identity as nothing else does. As God's child, the true you isn't defined by the labels on the outside of the man box. Indeed, God has built a man-of-God box, and it, not the world's expectations, should define who you are.

Consider that as a man of God, you're:

A coheir with Christ—you possess infinite riches (Rom. 8:17)

A man with eternal life—you possess infinite life (John 3:16)

A branch in the vine—you possess infinite resources (John 15:5)

Holy and blameless in Christ—you possess ultimate righteousness (Eph. 1:4)

A member of Christ's body—you have a crucial role (1 Cor. 12:18)

Christ's bride—you're loved unconditionally (Eph. 5:25)

Free of condemnation—you're completely forgiven (Rom. 8:1).

This partial list gives you a glimpse of how God views you. It describes your *true* identity in Christ. Jesus gently rebuked his followers for acting like abandoned orphans rather than God's children (Matt. 6:31–32). It's the orphan, who has no family identity or relationship with his father, that worries about food and clothing. Not the child!

Sometimes when I'm counseling a man who is locked in the man box, I wish I could give him a sledgehammer so he could break out and smash the box to bits. If the box were made of wood and held together by nails, it would be easier. But it's not. Instead, I challenge men—and I'm challenging you—to climb out of that box and refuse to get back in it again. Turn back to the description of the man box and read over the list. As you do so, say, "I don't have to be this or do that." And then tell yourself, "I'm God's child, and I just need to allow his life to flow through me."

That's all God wants from you. He's not asking you to go out on your own and try to accomplish something for him or your family. Instead, he wants you to enjoy him and allow him to live his life through you. You don't have to perform or achieve something for your heavenly Father to love and accept you. He already does!

Worry Ignores Reality

Understanding our new identity in Christ isn't something that happens all at once. It's a process—and I'll talk about that process in a later chapter. But once we begin to allow God to define who we are, we need to take the next step. We must consciously choose to remember that all God wants from us is faith. The author of Hebrews said, "Without faith it is impossible to please God" (Heb. 11:6). Did you catch that? All God wants from you is faith. Nothing more. Nothing less. Nothing in between. Just faith.

Pause for a moment and think about all the things that are stressing you out—marital problems, work responsibilities, financial difficulties, problems with your kids or parents, uncertain future, shameful past, health concerns, and anything else that comes to mind. All God wants you to do is hand them over to him and trust him to take care of it. No, that doesn't mean you don't have to do the best you can to solve the problem. But it does mean you don't need to sweat the outcome, because that's in God's hands.

To drive home our need to trust in God and not worry, Jesus pointed out to his listeners the futility of worry—and the stress that goes along with it. When we worry, we ignore a number of things.

1. *Worry ignores the logic of life (Matt. 6:25).* Which is of greater value, food and clothing or your body? The answer's obvious. Your body is of far greater worth. Doesn't it make sense that the God who has given you the greater gift won't neglect the lesser?

    Can you imagine a father buying his son a twenty-thousand-dollar car for graduation and then refusing to give him the keys? Of course not! Similarly, since God has given you the priceless gift of your body, he'll also give you all you need to sustain it.

    Every time we get stressed out and worry about how we'll provide for our families, we're ignoring this simple truth.

2. *Worry ignores the value of life (Matt. 6:26).* Have you ever heard of a sparrow dying of an ulcer? Of course

not. Why? Because they live a stress-free life. And they do it in spite of the fact that every morning when they wake up, they have no food in the pantry or savings in the bank. God cares for every sparrow. He makes sure each one has all the food it needs for each day he wants it to live.

The Lord's point was profound. He said, "Are you not much more valuable than they?" (Matt. 6:26). Every time you allow yourself to worry, you're saying that God cares for you less than he does a sparrow. As a child of God, such a thought is absurd. The next time you see a bird, allow it to be a reminder of God's eagerness to provide for you.

3. *Worry ignores its own limitations (Matt. 6:27).* Jesus asked his listeners a very simple question. He wanted to know if anyone had ever added a day to their life by worrying. When we worry, it's like sitting in a rocking chair—there's a lot of action but no progress. The next time you're getting stressed out, ask yourself, "Will all this stress really help solve the problem? Will it make my life better or longer?" Of course it won't.

4. *Worry ignores God's faithfulness.* Since God faithfully clothes the flowers of the field, will he be less faithful with us? He can't be. One of my favorite verses was written by the prophet Jeremiah after the fall of Jerusalem. With his world in ruins, the prophet said, "I remember my affliction and my wandering, the bitterness and the gall. I well remember them, and my soul is downcast within me. Yet this I call to mind and therefore I have hope: Because of the LORD's great love we are not consumed, for his compassions never fail. They are new every morning; great is your faithfulness" (Lam. 3:19–23).

When we allow ourselves to be stressed out, we're
ignoring God's promise to meet our needs. We're acting as though God could be unfaithful to us. And he
can't be!

5. *Worry ignores the present (Matt. 6:34).* When we
   worry, we focus on the future, which is seldom as bad
   as we fear it might be. I'm reminded of the story of
   the man who lived under continual stress because he
   worried about everything. One day a friend asked
   him, "John, have any of the tragedies you've worried
   about ever occurred?"

   John scratched his chin and smiled. "No, they
   haven't," he said. "I guess that proves my worrying
   really worked."

   Obviously, such logic isn't connected to reality.
   When we worry, we're placing tomorrow's clouds over
   today's sunshine. What a waste of good weather.

An Antidote for Stress

I have to tell you that I'm a real worrier. If things are going
well, I'll invent a potential problem just so I'll have something
to worry about. Of course, stress and worry go hand in hand.
Because I'm prone to suffer from stress like most men, I'm glad
Jesus not only pointed out the illogical nature of worry but gave
us an antidote. He said, "Seek first his kingdom and his righteousness, and all these things will be given to you as well"
(Matt. 6:33). *The Message* paraphrases the Lord's words. It says,
"Steep your life in God-reality, God-initiative, God-provisions.
Don't worry about missing out. You'll find all your everyday
human concerns met."[10]

Jesus exhorted his followers to avoid worry and stress by
focusing on God and his work. He urged them to trust in God.

I mentioned that stress is caused in part by misplaced faith. When we trust in ourselves to solve our problems and meet our needs, it creates stress. Why? Because we have limited resources. Instead of seeking to live up to the demands of the man box, we need to seek to know God better. We need to believe that his definition of our identity is the only legitimate one. And we should trust him to meet our needs.

As we connect with God and trust in him, we'll find our stress subsiding. When I was a kid growing up on an Ohio farm, I never worried about whether or not there would be food on the table or a roof over my head. Why? Because providing food and shelter was my dad's job, and I knew he'd never let me down. Now, if my earthly father could be trusted, how much more can our heavenly Father be trusted? Clearly, he'll never let us down.

Coming to grips with our identity in Christ, and learning to trust God to meet our needs, are crucial for dealing with stress. But there's another ingredient to this antidote. We need to connect with other men. As we feel safe with God, we'll discover he'll give us a sense of security that will free us up to talk more openly with other men. In return, they'll help us keep our perspective—and our focus on God. They'll encourage us to live in the man-of-God box instead of the man box.

I recently saw an article that illustrates the importance of relationships in diminishing stress. I like to run to keep myself in some semblance of shape. Well, maybe "like" is too strong a word, but I run anyway. Because of my interest in running, I occasionally read a runner's magazine to get the latest tips. A recent article pointed out the dangers of running at the wrong pace on an inflexible surface, like concrete. If a man runs on a hard surface too long, he can suffer a stress fracture in his legs. A stress fracture is a hairline crack in the bone of a runner's leg. If the person continues to run without proper rest, the stress fracture can actually get worse—a lot worse. The bone can shatter.

By the time I'd read that far, the writer had my attention. I wanted to know how I could prevent a stress fracture. He said the key is to run at different speeds, on a variety of surfaces— asphalt, grass, an indoor track, a dirt road—and to allow for periodic "downtime." And then came the shocker—*running with a friend helps prevent stress fractures, by keeping a runner from overdoing it.*

I couldn't help but make the connection with the rest of life. I find that many men are running at breakneck speed in their lives, without proper downtime, and consequently causing stress fractures in their emotional, spiritual, physical, psychological, and marital lives. They eventually end up shattering their lives and those around them. Many men need downtime. But I've found that few men will take such time without having a few "running mates" to encourage them to do so. I know I won't. If we're going to cope with stress, we need to focus on God and cultivate close friendships with other men.

A FINAL DANGER

So far, we've seen two major consequences of our hiding. But there's a third result that I believe can be the most devastating of all if we do not come out of hiding. It addresses the very core of who we are as men. You'll see what I mean in the next chapter.

DISCUSSION QUESTIONS

1. Stress causes problems physically, emotionally, relationally and spiritually. Some physical effects were listed. What are the effects emotionally, spiritually and relationally?

2. How did you come out on the general stress symptoms check-list on page 46–7? Did some of the items surprise you as being stress related?

3. As a group, take a box (maybe even a refrigerator size one!) and write on the outside as many messages as you can come up with that are "man messages." Jesus used physical symbols to remind his children of his presence. Use this "man box" to symbolically remind yourself to be open and vulnerable. Make another box your God box. Put Scripture verses on and inside the box. For instance, on the outside of the man box may be the message "big boys don't cry," while on the God box is the verse about Jesus weeping over Jerusalem or at Lazarus' grave.

4. What "man messages" were you given as a child? How have they carried over into your adult life? How do these messages define your identity?

5. Dr. Cooper wrote, "You don't have to perform or achieve something for our heavenly Father to love and accept you." How does that make you feel? Anxious? Relieved? Disappointed? Grateful? Why?

6. What steps can you take to hand things over to God?

7. In the Sermon on the Mount, Jesus addressed such "heavy sins" as adultery, murder and spiritual pride. Why do you think Jesus added worry in here?

CHAPTER 4

Meaninglessness

A buddy of mine had rented a beach house on the Texas coast for a family vacation. It was an annual affair that always included building a giant sand castle. This particular summer he wanted to construct one so big that his kids would never forget it. He knew something as massive as the pyramids wasn't possible. But he figured they could build one the size of a small shed.

With that in mind, he hiked to the flat Texas beach early in the morning, carrying a rusty shovel over his shoulder. One of his sons pushed an old wheelbarrow, while the other carried a water bucket. The tide was out, so they had plenty of beach to pick from. Once they had all agreed on a location, the work began.

The first thing they did was dig a hole in the sand for the foundation. After cleaning the beach of stones and shells, they dumped a wheelbarrow full of them into the foundation hole— this baby was going to stand tall and strong. On the foundation, they constructed a wall out of boards. Finally they piled on wheelbarrow after wheelbarrow of sand.

When the three had shaped the sand into the form of a castle, with towers and walls and gates, they stood back and admired their masterpiece. The castle stood over five feet tall. The kids could actually run around inside its walls. And the moat guarded it from a surprise attack on any side. One couple that strolled by commented on the huge castle they had built.

As the hot day wore on, the tide began to creep in. The first wave to hit the castle washed away a few inches of sand. The next wave, a big one, crashed over the wall, melting it away. One of the boys squealed when the third wave washed away the boards. In no time at all, the boards floated away and the rocks disappeared into the wet sand. By sunset there was no trace of their sand castle. The Padre Island beach was as flat and barren as it had been that morning when they arrived.

The better I get to know myself and other men, the more I'm convinced that because we're in hiding, there's something we fear more than poverty, illness, or injury. In a sense, it's like our fear of death. We know that one day we'll die, but we don't think about dying all the time or we couldn't function. This fear is like that. It's there just under the surface of our consciousness. It's the fear that our lives won't matter. A fear that after we've lived and died, life will go on as if we had never been there—just like a sand castle.

THE SEARCH FOR SIGNIFICANCE

I remember when my father died. One day he was there, the next day he was gone. And life went on. Just like a sand castle on the beach. For a few hours the castle stands tall and then it's gone. The beach is the same as it was before but the castle isn't there anymore. People walking on the shore won't even know the castle was ever there.

I know that someday this will happen to me. A few days, months, or years after I'm gone, I'll be forgotten. It will be as if I'd never lived. I fear, as does every man, that my life will not have mattered. Regardless of how much I accomplish or how much I possess, I want my life to count.

Others have expressed their struggle for significance. Mark Twain said, "A myriad of men are born, they labor and sweat and struggle; they squabble and scold and fight; they scramble for little mean advantages over each other; age creeps upon them; infirmities follow; those they love are taken from them and the joy of life is turned to aching grief. It (the release) comes at last—the only unpoisoned gift earth ever had for them—and they vanish from a world where they were of no consequence—a world which will lament them for a day and forget them forever."

Viktor Frankl noted, "Clinics are crowded with people suffering from a new kind of neurosis, a sense of total and ultimate meaninglessness of life."

Even basketball star Sir Charles Barkley once said, in a 1994 television interview, that the purpose of his life—his reason to exist—was to win an NBA title. That's a great goal, but does it qualify as something that will give his life lasting meaning? Hardly! It's not a purpose that will last a lifetime. And what if he should achieve it? What then?

As a therapist, I'm trained to help people unravel their emotional and psychological problems. But helping a man overcome his sense of meaninglessness is beyond me. It's beyond any psychologist. Why? Because it's a spiritual issue. It has to do with a man's relationship with God—and other people. Until we come out of hiding and connect with God and other men at a deeper level, we're going to continue to feel empty inside. No matter what we have or do, it won't fill the hole. It won't satisfy. It won't give our lives meaning.

The search for significance, or meaning, isn't new. Solomon addressed it thousands of years ago in the book of Ecclesiastes. Within the lines of this short book, he repeatedly raised the issue of life's meaning. What's astounding about the book of Ecclesiastes is that Solomon raised the issues in a cynical, despondent tone. His words hardly sound like those of a godly man.

For instance, in the opening lines he wrote, "Generations come and generations go, but the earth remains forever" (Eccl. 1:4). Later he said, "Man's fate is like that of the animals; the same fate awaits them both: As one dies, so dies the other. All have the same breath; man has no advantage over the animal" (Eccl. 3:19).

Those are radical words, words that reveal the heart of a man in hiding, a man who struggled long and hard with the ultimate meaning of life and tried to find the answer alone. Solomon's words aren't merely philosophical; they describe the story of his life. In his search for life's meaning, he utilized his vast wealth and wisdom to see what, if anything, would give his life purpose. Time and again he expressed frustration and disappointment. Yet the book isn't one of despair but of hope. In the end he found the secret that gives life meaning. And he shared the secret with us.

In his excellent book *When All You've Ever Wanted Isn't Enough*, Harold Kushner tells the story of a man who went for a walk in the forest and got lost. The man tried to find the way back to town, following one path after another, but none of them led out. Then he suddenly encountered another hiker walking through the forest. He cried out, "Thank God for another human being! Can you show me the way back to town?"

The other man replied, "No. I'm lost, too. But we can help each other in this way: We can tell each other which paths we have already tried and been disappointed in. That'll help us find the one that will lead out."[1]

Before Solomon directed us out of the forest of meaninglessness, he warned us about the false paths and dead ends. Only when we learn which paths will not give life meaning will we be prepared to take the right one.

KNOWLEDGE

It's important to realize that Solomon's evaluation focused on life "under the sun" (Eccl. 1:3). He viewed life from the perspective of a man in hiding. He looked at life from a human, not a divine, perspective. As he did so, he concluded that everything is "utterly meaningless" (v. 2). Viewed through the eyes of a man disconnected from God and other people, life has no permanence or purpose.

To illustrate his point, he mentioned nature. The sun races across the sky every day, only to start its journey all over again the next morning (v. 5). The wind blows in circles and returns to the spot where it began. Water flows to the sea, returns to the sky as clouds, falls to the ground as rain, and runs into rivers again. Everything's the same. Nothing really changes. It all seemed so meaningless to Solomon.

And what about the accumulation of wisdom, or knowledge? All human knowledge is partial. It's limited. I'll never forget watching the launch of the space shuttle *Challenger*. It represented the brightest and best of our country. The greatest scientists of our day used their skills to build it. Yet on that tragic day in 1986, *Challenger* self-destructed with tragic results. Why? Because a single O-ring had been damaged by ice. When I heard that announcement, I was stunned. The most brilliant scientists in the world had their masterpiece blown apart by a frozen O-ring. That's the problem with wisdom "under the sun." It's only partial.

Solomon didn't come to that conclusion quickly. He learned everything he could about business, engineering, and politics. If he lived today, he might say, "I earned doctorates from Harvard in business, engineering, and politics. I rubbed shoulders with the brightest. I mastered the most complex concepts. When all was said and done, I still felt empty."

I can't help but laugh when I think about the story of four people—a pastor, an expectant mother, a Boy Scout, and a brilliant scientist—who were flying in a plane. Just as the plane reached cruising altitude, the pilot stepped into the passenger section of the craft and announced that the engines had failed and the plane was about to crash. As he slipped on a parachute, he told them there were three additional parachutes in the closet behind them.

A moment after the pilot leaped from the plane, the scientist raced to the closet, opened the door, and grabbed the three parachutes. He gave one to the Boy Scout and said, "You have your whole life ahead of you. Put this on." He tossed one to the young woman and said, "You're really two people, so you should get one." As he slipped his arms into the shoulder straps of the third parachute, he said, "I'm the most brilliant man alive. The world needs me, so I'll use the last parachute."

As the scientist jumped through the door into the open air, the pastor told the other two, "Go ahead and jump. God will take care of me."

The Boy Scout looked at him and said, "Relax, pastor. The most brilliant man in the world just jumped out of the plane wearing my backpack."

As smart as that man may have been, he only possessed partial knowledge. That's why no man will ever find the true meaning to life through knowledge.

PLEASURE

If there's one word that describes the primary pursuit of our society, it would be "pleasure." We seek it in our work, recreation, cars, and boats. We hope to find it through alcohol, drugs, and sex. Indeed, today men feel more pressure than ever before to be "good" at sex. We've been brainwashed into believing that to be healthy, growing individuals, we'll do it more, be better at it, and derive more pleasure from it. And if we don't, we're missing out.

Imagine for a moment that you had more money than Bill Gates. And suppose you decided to use your financial resources to test pleasure and find out what would truly satisfy. That's exactly what Solomon did. He tested laughter but it didn't satisfy. Next he experimented with aged wines to discover their charm. His experience with wine wasn't that of an alcoholic trying to deaden emotional pain. Rather, it was the experimentation of a genius trying to discover if the taste and pleasure of wine would satisfy his desire for meaning. When the wine didn't satisfy, he tried to find satisfaction through the expression of his creative genius. He built beautiful gardens and lakes and amassed a fortune in gold and silver.

Solomon stood at the top of the heap and looked down at the rest of the world. He'd accomplished more than anyone. He possessed everything a man could want (Eccl. 2:4–9). Yet he wanted more.

When he discovered that possessions couldn't fill the hole in his heart, he pursued the sensual pleasures found with women. King Solomon didn't experiment with one or two women. No way! He acquired a harem. The king had seven hundred wives and three hundred concubines (1 Kings 11:3). A thousand women lived to satisfy his every fantasy. He could have them at any time and in any number. And they were the most beautiful women alive. Yet he was bored.

As Solomon surveyed all he'd acquired and experienced, he concluded, "All of it is meaningless, a chasing after the wind" (Eccl. 2:17).

When I consider Solomon's experience, I'm reminded of an old episode of *The Twilight Zone* that told of an East Coast gangster who died. Following his death, the ill-mannered hoodlum found himself in a beautiful penthouse in a high-rise gambling casino. He soon realized things couldn't be better. In this new world he ruled like a king. Every time he gambled, he won. A beautiful woman laughed at his jokes and showered him with affection. He had everything he thought would satisfy.

Over time he found himself bored. Always winning and always getting what he wanted had eroded his pleasure. He craved a challenge and asked the gray-haired attendant if God hadn't sent him to heaven by mistake. The servant informed the man that God hadn't sent him to heaven. He was in hell!

That episode could've been drawn from the life of Solomon. He found that all the pleasure in the world wouldn't satisfy his longing for purpose and meaning. When the laugher died and the pleasure passed—he felt empty. Life seemed meaningless.

WORK

Since pleasure couldn't give his life meaning, Solomon looked to his work. Have you ever noticed that the people who say success doesn't satisfy are always the ones who have it? I certainly have. And I've thought that it's easy for them to say success isn't important, since they've already made it to the top.

Why do we feel that way? Because in our society, a young boy learns to value himself in terms of achievements, successes, and victories. The message is driven home to him constantly, through direct and indirect communication. His dad calls him "my son" when he runs faster, speaks better, wins a game, reads earlier, gets a higher grade, scores a touchdown, wins a fight, or does anything else to show his superiority over other young boys.[2]

Occasionally a boy will be reminded that he can't let up. He can't rest on past victories. He lives in a world that only applauds winners. Losers get no sympathy. Like the television commercial during the 1996 Summer Olympics that said, "Silver medals aren't won. Gold medals are lost." The message is clear—you don't win second place, you lose first place.

In that context men are driven to win. We're driven to succeed. And we're driven to work longer and harder so we can succeed. Well, suppose you do succeed at work. Will your work and the success it brings give your life lasting meaning?

Solomon said it won't. Why? Because whatever you build with your hands, you'll one day hand off to another person, who'll destroy it. I know of a man who built a national restaurant chain. He poured the best days of his life into that business. Eventually he sold it to a major corporation. Within five years most of the restaurants had closed. Why? Because while the leaders of that large corporation knew how to build and manage hotels, they didn't know how to run restaurants. The business empire built by one man was dismantled by others.

How did Solomon view such an experience? He said, "What does a man get for all the toil and anxious striving with which he labors under the sun? All his days his work is pain and grief; even at night his mind does not rest. This too is meaningless" (Eccl. 2:22–23).

All the hard work and restless nights result in nothing. Zip. Zilch. Zero.

Listen to the words of Solomon. When we hide from God and other people, we're destined to search for life's meaning in all the wrong places. Places like our work. No matter how important your job might be, you'll never find lasting meaning in your job. It can't possibly fill the hole in your heart.

RICHES

Neither can money. The famed Irish poet and dramatist Oscar Wilde once wrote, "In this world there are only two tragedies. One is not getting what one wants, and the other is getting it." No matter how much wealth a person accumulates, it won't satisfy. The list of wealthy people who have self-destructed grows tragically long. When the veneer is stripped away, even the rich long for something more, something money can't give them.

But suppose you were lucky enough to make a fortune. Solomon did. And then he was faced with two troubling realities—and they're similar to those associated with our work. The first was that those he would leave his wealth to would eventually squander it. Not only will a man's empire be dismantled, so will the wealth he acquires (Eccl. 2:21). The rich don't always get richer, because those who inherit a fortune don't always possess the skill and drive of their parents.

Writing in *Forbes* magazine, investment counselor David Dreman noted that most large fortunes diminish and sometimes disappear in only two or three generations. Even the most brilliant financial minds can't guarantee that their fortune will survive a single generation after they die. Solomon said it's folly to devote your life to building something that can be torn down by those who come after you.

The second problem Solomon faced is that the money doesn't always wait a generation before it disappears. A fortune that took a lifetime to build can quickly vanish due to some misfortune. John Connally was one of the great governors of Texas. He was respected as a shrewd businessman and politician. But I remember watching television one evening when the news showed him auctioning off his possessions. Why? Because he needed the money to pay off his creditors. Connally lost everything during the recession of the late seventies and early eighties. So did a lot of other wealthy Texas businessmen. None of them foresaw the oil crisis and the effect it would have on the Texas economy. Even the rich can lose everything.

Have you ever noticed the eagle with outstretched wings on the back of a dollar bill? I think it's there to remind us that money can quickly fly away. In fact, in Proverbs 23:5 Solomon said, "Cast but a glance at riches, and they are gone, for they will surely sprout wings and fly off to the sky like an eagle."

It would be easy to misunderstand Solomon and think he viewed money as evil. He didn't. Nor did any other biblical writer. Some of the greatest men in the Bible were wealthy. The issue isn't possessing money but loving money and looking to it for meaning in life. Why expect something to give your life purpose, when it can suddenly disappear? Solomon realized that danger and therefore said that the pursuit of wealth is meaningless.

If knowledge, pleasure, work, and wealth didn't give Solomon's life lasting meaning because they were transitory and incomplete, only one possibility remained. If this last path led him down a dead-end street, life would in fact be futile and meaningless. In his final throw of the dice, Solomon turned to God. He looked for meaning to life above the sun rather than under it.

Remember, until now Solomon had been hiding from God. He'd been relationally disconnected from the most important relationship in life. Finally he sought a connection with God. And so must we.

MEETING THE LOCKSMITH

Many people who read the book of Ecclesiastes miss Solomon's dramatic conclusion. It's so simple, they read over it without catching what he meant. He said, "Now all has been heard; here is the conclusion of the matter: Fear God and keep his commandments" (Eccl. 12:13).

All men would like the key that unlocks the mysteries of life. Solomon wanted that. And he searched high and low for the key. But God wouldn't give it to him through knowledge, pleasure, work, or money. Instead, God did something better. He gave Solomon himself. We want the key that unlocks life's meaning; instead God offers us a relationship with the Locksmith.

Meaning isn't found by chasing after success or pleasure. It's not found in accumulating money or toys. True meaning in life is found when we come out of hiding and make a connection with the One who loves us. The One who accepts us. The One who infuses us with himself.

We're to "fear God and keep his commandments." When Solomon urged us to "fear" God, he wasn't talking about the terror a child has around an abusive parent, or the uptight respect a new recruit has for a tough drill sergeant. When we fear God, we stand in awe of him. We revere him.

Several years ago I visited the Oregon coast with Bill Perkins. As we drove south along the coastline, I was spellbound by the massive rocks that towered out from the water. When we were about fifteen miles south of the resort town of Cannon Beach, Bill pulled the car over at a viewpoint high above the water. Along the edge of the parking lot was a two-foot-high stone wall. Bill climbed over the wall and said, "Follow me. I'm going to show you my favorite spot on the Oregon coast."

The path was hidden and seldom traveled. As I followed Bill, I felt a bit apprehensive, because on either side was a high cliff. When I say high, I mean way up there. Fortunately, after we had walked twenty yards or so, the trail took us between some sort of vegetation that was eight or nine feet high—tall enough to obscure our view in every direction.

When we had walked a quarter of a mile, we suddenly exited the vegetation and stood at the very end of a point that protruded several hundred yards out over the ocean. Behind and below us to the north were towering cliffs made of rock that looked like layered black slate. Portions of the rock cliff stuck out in a perpendicular angle from the rest of the cliff, and I could see what looked like giant keyholes in the black slate. Towering waves crashed into the rocks and sent white foamy spray through the keyholes.

The sensation I experienced at that moment merged both fear and fascination. I was captured by the power and beauty of the waves and rocks. Yet I knew that if I took one false step, I'd plummet to my death. Even so, I wanted to stand as close as I could to the cliff's edge so I could see the spectacular show of power and beauty below.

After standing there silently for a while, Bill and I erupted in praise to the God who had created that masterpiece. Never have I sung "How Great Thou Art" with such feeling. In that moment I stood in awe of nature and God. I experienced fear, pleasure, and respect. I admired the beauty of that spot, yet I respected the danger of getting too close to the edge.

I think that sensation is similar to the kind of "fear" we're to have toward God. When we fear God, we stand in awe of his beauty, power, and love. We're not flippant—we're respectful. And when we fear God, we want to get as close to him as we can. Why? Because his beauty, majesty, and love draw us. And we want to obey him. Why? Because his power and beauty flow through us, creating both the desire and the will to keep his commandments.

I later took Nancy to that spot on the Oregon coast. I wanted her to share my experience. Like me, she was hesitant to walk down the path. Yet like me, she found it well worth the hike and the risk.

I've often thought that this is what we do with God. When we connect with him, we want others to share our experience. And as we make that connection together, something happens inside us. In that moment we experience eternity. And we discover something that gives our life meaning. Something that gives us permanence.

Of course, making that connection with God and other men may seem risky. And it is. It will involve coming out of hiding. It will mean running the risk of being seen by others, who might reject you. But the payoff's worth it. It's better than the spectacular view from a cliff. When you come out of hiding, you'll discover why God created you. And then, regardless of what you possess or achieve, you'll know you have relationships that are true and deep. And you'll know your life counts.

If that's what you want—and I know it is—turn the page. With part 2, we begin the journey that will allow you to come out of hiding and find your purpose. It's a journey that will enable you to stand shoulder to shoulder with other men of purpose.

DISCUSSION QUESTIONS

1. What gives your life meaning? Is it something Solomon addresses in Ecclesiastes?
2. Discuss the difference between goals and a purpose.
3. How does meaninglessness tie in with addiction?
4. Dr. Cooper wrote that ". . . a young boy learns to value himself in terms of achievements, successes, and victories." How does that message translate over in the church, directly and indirectly?
5. Read Ecclesiastes 2:21–23. Compare this with Matthew 6:19–21 and 1 Peter 1:3–5. What is our inheritance?
6. An advertisement during the Olympics ran "Silver medals aren't won. Gold medals are lost." Compare this message with Isaiah 53. How do we best bear the image of Christ?

PART TWO

Moving toward Brotherhood

5. Facing Reality

To enter into accountability, a man must be willing to come out of hiding and face the truth about himself. He must be convinced that facing reality, no matter how painful, is better than living a secret life. Then he'll be able to grieve his losses and embrace the hope that God will make him complete.

6. In Process

A man moving toward accountability recognizes that he hasn't spiritually arrived but is on a journey. He also knows this is true of other men. Since this is the case, he realizes that reaching the destination isn't as important as how he gets there. Since he knows he's in process, he's willing to share his weaknesses with others.

7. The Huddle

A man who enters into accountability believes that a team is stronger than an individual. He knows that the team will give him the support he needs to face the realities about himself and life. He also knows that he'll not be abandoned, and he's made a commitment not to abandon others. He believes in the adage "One for all and all for one."

CHAPTER 5

Facing Reality

"My name is Bond, James Bond." I don't know of anyone who hasn't heard that famous line from 007, the British spy. Those words immediately conjure up an image of a man who is in *total* control of his world. Nothing takes him by surprise. In every situation that comes his way, he not only survives—he conquers. My wife, Nancy, has often said that Bond's life is like Murphy's law in reverse. If anything can go right, it will.

For instance, the latest Bond movie is called *Goldeneye*. The first scene contains one of the most incredible stunts I've ever witnessed in all my movie watching—and let me tell you, that's a lot. The movie starts with Bond hurling himself off a dam that must be several hundred feet high. He's tied to a bungee cord, and just as it stretches to yank him upward, he pulls out a miniature crossbow and shoots a steel arrow into the top of a small door at the bottom of the dam, where he gains entrance. Split-second timing's required, but of course he makes it.

Once he's inside the dam, we discover that it pulls double duty as a hideout for top-secret ammunition held by the Soviets. Dispatching several bad guys, Bond teams up with his partner, 006. They begin to plant plastic explosives to destroy the dam, but of course an alarm goes off and they are hopelessly surrounded. Bond's partner gets shot, and 007 figures he'd better advance the timers on the explosives so he can blow up the place sooner. Somehow he then manages to escape the hundred or so men who are after him, and he makes it back to the top.

A plane happens to be taking off down a runway on the other side of the dam. Bond punches out a Russian and steals his motorcycle, hoping to catch the plane just before it takes off. Dodging bullets and fighting Russians, he keeps pursuing the plane. It takes off, and Bond seems destined to be caught. But no! He revs up his bike and runs it full speed to the runway's edge, which is a cliff, and rides the motorcycle out over the abyss. Mind you, he doesn't have a parachute on at this time. Racing like a bullet after the plane, he somehow catches it, throws out the pilot, and gets behind the controls. But it's not over (I bet you knew that). The plane's in a severe nose dive and heading for a mountain. Bond uses all his strength and—again with perfect timing—pulls the plane out of its dive and escapes unharmed. Oh, by the way, the ammunition depot was blown to bits. Mission accomplished. Truly, this is Murphy's law backward.

I believe that all men would like to think that on a good day they would handle life as securely and assuredly as Bond. But that's a movie and *we* live in reality, where Murphy's law is—well, Murphy's law.

I realized how little control I had one week when I had a writing deadline to meet. I'd finished a lot of good work, and then it happened—out of nowhere a power surge came, and all my week's work was gone. I had a surge protector and had even backed up my data, but somehow all of it was lost. I did everything I could to retrieve it, but I eventually had to start over. Also, the circuits in my computer were blown, and I had to take it in to get it repaired. I was without my computer for a week. Murphy was right—if anything can go wrong, it will.

The first step a man must take if he's going to experience dynamic relationships is to realize he's not James Bond. He must face the reality that he really does not have control of his life. When my computer crashed, I felt totally helpless. There wasn't anything I could do. I was not in control, and I needed to get help if I was going to get done what I needed to accomplish. I had to face the fact that I could not do it on my own.

As a counselor, I've found that true healing and healthy relationships depend on how willing a person is to face reality. The foundation for any type of recovery lies in recognizing just how little control we actually have concerning our lives, and how much we truly need others.

Alcoholics Anonymous has twelve steps a person must adhere to for recovery, and I believe there are similar steps a man must follow if he's to come out of isolation and develop "shoulder-to-shoulder relationships." I call them the Eight Steps to Building Brotherhood. Let's take a look at three of them in this chapter.

1. I Am Powerless and Cannot Control My Life

There's a story about a little boy who was helping his father stack some wood cut from a fallen tree. The little boy reached down and tried to pick up a piece of wood that was just about as big as he was. He grunted and groaned and then stopped, exhausted. He could not move it. He said to his father, "Daddy, I can't move it."

The man answered, "Well, Son, are you using all your strength?"

The little boy said, "Yes." Not to be outdone by this piece of wood, the little boy braced himself and grabbed it with absolute resolution. He grunted and groaned and barely lifted the piece of wood, only to drop it. He began to cry and said, "Daddy, I can't lift it."

His father answered, "Son, are you using all your strength?"
The little boy, wiping his eyes, said, "Yes, Daddy."
His dad replied, "No, you're not, Son. You haven't asked me."
"Daddy, will you help me?"
"Sure, Son."
Now the log was lifted with ease, because the boy was using all his strength.

Too often we men fail to use all our strength—our brothers in Christ who are standing there waiting to pitch in and help. Usually we become utterly exhausted trying to bear loads twice our size, because of a myth we've bought into. It's the *c* word—otherwise known as "control."

It's a myth to think we're in control. The truth is, the best we can do is manage. Even Jesus said, in Matthew 6:34, "Do not worry about tomorrow, for tomorrow will worry about itself. Each day has enough trouble of its own."

If a man's going to come out of isolation and into brotherhood, he first of all must admit he needs help from his brothers. Every man every day faces the onslaught of a culture that attacks his masculinity—emotionally, spiritually, psychologically, and even physically. If he's not careful, he can begin to get traumatized by it. Yet it seems to take extreme consequences to get a man to cry uncle. I've found that for a man to come out of denial and face the reality of needing others, he often needs to hit bottom. The term "hitting bottom" refers to an event in which a person literally faces the fact that they can no longer keep doing what they have been doing and survive. Tragically, many men must have such an experience before they'll say they need help.

I saw it happen to one of my friends. His name's Ned. He's one of the most responsible and caring men I've ever met, yet he hit a brick wall in his life. You see, Ned suffers from chronic back pain. He has had two operations, and there is not a day that goes by in which he doesn't feel pain. A good day is when he hurts for only a few hours and not all day. The pain got pretty bad, so Ned went to his physician for help. The doctor gave him some muscle relaxers that were supposed to help ease the pain. They eased the pain, but they also caused him to begin to withdraw from life. He would take as many as seven or eight a day. His family, especially his wife, could always tell if he was on a muscle relaxer, because his personality would change. He would become lethargic and zombielike in his behavior. In fact, his wife began to confront him, but he kept saying the doctor told him they weren't addictive.

This went on for about six months. Ned told me that he'd ceased to live life and was now just surviving it. He would tell his doctor that he probably needed medication that wasn't so severe, but the doctor kept telling him the muscle relaxers weren't addictive. If you can't trust your doctor, who can you trust? Finally it got so bad that Ned's wife threatened to leave, especially after she heard him call a coworker and say over and over, "Man, this is a trip." He didn't remember the phone conversation. To Ned's credit, he did try to stop for a while on his own, but soon the pain would be too much and he would be back on the pills again. Even when his wife would ask, "Are you off the muscle relaxers?" he would be untruthful and say he was doing much better. Finally, after much prayer on Ned's wife's part, God intervened.

You see, Ned got a major sinus infection and had to go to a clinic close to his house. The physician he saw happened to be a Christian. Ned asked for a certain kind of medication to help clear the infection. The request seemed unusual to the doctor, but he decided to give Ned a small amount. He handed Ned a prescription for fifteen capsules. Well, Ned took it and while going to the pharmacy changed the one to a four. He handed the prescription to the pharmacist, who filled it. Right after

Ned left the store, the pharmacist got a call from the doctor at the clinic, who said, "I've thought about Ned's prescription and would like you to increase it to twenty capsules."

The pharmacist said, "Well, you don't need to, because the prescription was for forty-five, and I just gave it to him."

The doctor immediately called Ned's wife and told her what had happened. He asked her to confront Ned and bring him immediately back to the clinic to talk.

When Ned opened the garage door, his wife said, "I have only one question to ask—did you just now change a prescription to get more medication?"

Ned broke down crying and said, "Yes. Thank God you caught me." They went to the Christian physician, who proceeded to help Ned face his pain and get off the addictive medication. Ned and his wife say that God answered prayer by lovingly catching Ned in a lie and by providing a Christian physician who would support him in recovering from his addiction.

Ned went to therapy and gave these reasons why he kept doing the pills:

1. "I thought I could quit at any time."
2. "I figured I would be less than a man if I admitted I couldn't stop and asked for help."
3. "Things weren't really that bad."

In truth, things had been very bad. Ned would later say, "Hitting bottom was the best thing I could've done, because I would've destroyed myself and lost my family otherwise."

Ned and his family are now growing closer. Ned readily admits his need for help and has continued to receive counseling. He has an accountability partner to help him stay on track. In fact, Ned now knows what many men need to realize—God never intended us to keep secrets, because it isolates us from others. Ned found that it's when we let the secret out and ask others to help that we truly begin to experience the joy of life. Knowing there are others who are willing to help us "bear our burdens" will help us hold up and not fold up when the storms of life come our way.

But maybe you're not convinced. Let me give you an example of a man from the Scriptures who would not ask for help, had to be in control, and in the process lost everything— even his own life. His name was Saul. Saul was chosen by God to be the king of Israel. He started his reign by defeating the Ammonites, but after that victory it was all downhill. In 1 Samuel 13 a Philistine invasion threatened Israel. Instead of waiting for the priest Samuel to come and offer the sacrifices before God, Saul decided to take matters into his own hands and offer them himself. This was clearly against God's command in 1 Samuel 10:8. You see, Saul felt he didn't need Samuel. He was perfectly capable of doing this himself, and God would just have to understand.

There were three results of Saul's stubborn independence. These results are as true today as they were for Saul, and if you don't believe it, just look at what happened in the past whenever you tried to take matters into your own hands. The first result is found in 1 Samuel 13.8–9: *By needing to be in control and not depending on Samuel, Saul turned directly away from God's word.* Saul clearly disregarded what he knew to be God's command. There's no question the circumstances were bleak, in that the people were leaving and Saul was afraid of losing his army. But God had already promised he would meet Saul's needs if Saul would trust him and depend on Samuel. One thing I learned when growing up on our farm in Ohio was that our focus determines our response. I learned this through the carpentry work I had to do. I had to hammer thousands of nails, and one thing I learned was that you always watch the nail, never the thumb holding the nail. Similarly, if our focus is on Christ and his word, we won't miss the mark or move ahead of it. We can depend on him. But if we must be in control, we'll resort to whatever seems expedient to meet the need of the moment.

The second result was this: *Not depending on God and his partner Samuel led Saul to deception* (vv. 10–12). Saul took on what I call a jungle-rules mentality—doing whatever it takes to get our needs met, even if it means rationalizing our behavior. Remember, rationalization is a key defense mechanism men will use to justify the need to be in control. We try to convince ourselves, others, and even the Lord that we had to do what we did. This is exactly what Saul did. He excused his behavior by pointing out that the people were scattered, Samuel didn't show up when he expected him, and the Philistines had a large army. On the surface these look like pretty good reasons, and we might have taken the same step Saul did if we had been in his shoes. What was wrong was that Saul's act was a direct violation of God's word. The result was that instead of admitting his error and humbling himself before God and Samuel and thus indicating he truly needed them, Saul rationalized his actions. Notice that he didn't claim to have misunderstood the instructions. Like Saul, if we are not careful, we can become hardhearted and slip into the defense mechanism of rationalization.

The third result was: *Needing to be in control made Saul toss away a potential blessing from God* (vv. 13–14). The same can happen to us. We may end up with less than God's best for us—or worse, nothing at all. Saul's actions lost him the kingdom and eventually his own life, all due to the fact that he needed to be in control and would not depend on God and those whom God had placed around him to help him along. Proverbs 26:12 says, "Do you see a man wise in his own eyes? There is more hope for a fool than for him." I believe it's pride that keeps us from saying, "I need help." It's when we can lay down our pride and realize our desperateness that we'll be able to begin the journey out of isolation and into brotherhood. Eugene Peterson, in his paraphrase of Matthew 5:3–4, says, "You're blessed when you're at the end of your rope. With less of you there's more of God and his rule. You're blessed when you feel you've lost what is most dear to you. Only then can you be embraced by the One most dear to you" (*The Message*).

Surrendering control is not easy, because it sounds like quitting or giving up. And that goes against our nature for striving, overcoming, and competing. As men, we are to believe that only sissies have weaknesses. We may rationalize away a few weaknesses in ourselves, but to say, "I'm powerless and can't manage my life" is truly difficult. Yet the Scriptures promise us that "God gives grace to the humble but opposes the proud" (*The Message*). The more a man humbles himself before God, the more he can count on a special measure of grace from God.

2. I NEED GOD TO FIX ME— TO GIVE ME A PROPER PERSPECTIVE

> Humpty Dumpty sat on the wall.
> Humpty Dumpty had a great fall.
> All the king's horses and all the king's men
> Couldn't put Humpty back together again.

But the King can. Hebrews 11:6 says, "Without faith it is impossible to please him: for he that cometh to God must believe that he is, and that he is a rewarder of them that diligently seek him" (KJV). There's no question that when we realize that all we have left is God, we discover that God is enough—the King can put our life back together again.

London businessman Lindsay Clegg told the story of a warehouse property he was selling. The building had been empty for months and needed repairs. Vandals had damaged the doors, smashed the windows, and strewn trash around the interior. As he showed a prospective buyer the property, Clegg took pains to say that he would replace the broken windows, bring in a crew to correct any structural damage, and clean out the garbage. "Forget about the repairs," the buyer said. "When I buy this place, I'm going to build something completely different. I don't want the building; I want the site." Compared with the renovation God has in mind, our efforts to improve our own lives are as trivial as sweeping a warehouse slated for a wrecking ball. When we become God's, the old life is over (2 Cor. 5:17). He makes all things new. All he wants is the site and permission to build.

It's when I decide to let God run my life that I finally see life in perspective. So much of life depends on our perspective, the way we view something. The term literally suggests looking through . . . seeing clearly. One who views life in perspective has the capacity to see things in their true relationship or relative importance. They can see the big picture. They can distinguish the incidental from the essential, the temporal from eternal, the partial from the whole, the trees from the forest. They have the ability to focus on what's left, not what's lost. If I face reality, I can grab life by the throat and live it, because "I am crucified with Christ: nevertheless I live; yet not I, but Christ liveth in me: and the life which I now live in the flesh I live by the faith of the Son of God, who loved me, and gave himself for me" (Gal. 2:20 KJV). I can see life clearly and live it fully because he's in control. This allows me to put even the most negative circumstances into a positive perspective, because "*all* things work together for good to them that love God" (Rom. 8:28 KJV, emphasis added).

This puts me in mind of a story about a young preacher who had just graduated from seminary. He took a small pastorate in a rural area of Georgia. Since the church was small, it didn't take him long to learn who the real "power brokers" were. They were two deacons—Deacon Jones and Deacon Smith. Now, each of these deacons had special talents, but Deacon Jones had an unusual talent. His talent was making the best peach brandy in the area. I don't know what denomination this church belonged to, but apparently everyone was encouraged to use their gifts.

Well, the preacher decided he wanted a little taste of this famous brandy, so he made a pastoral call on Deacon Jones. When he arrived at the deacon's house, they exchanged the usual pleasantries, and then the preacher asked if he could have a little taste of the deacon's brandy. The deacon said, "Preacher, no way am I going to cause you to sin. I can't do it."

"Look," the preacher replied, "I don't have a problem with alcohol. I just want a little sip of your brandy to say that I've had some."

"OK, but on the condition that you tell the congregation you had some of my brandy this Sunday," the deacon said.

The preacher thought for a moment and then said, "I can do that." So the deacon poured him a little and the preacher drank it down. It was just as smooth as he'd heard.

Well, sure enough, Sunday morning arrived, and the preacher began to make some announcements. He said, "I just want to thank Sister Smith for those apple pies. They were really tasty. And I want to thank Sister Johnson for baby-sitting the kids so my wife and I could have a night out. And I especially want to thank Deacon Jones for those peaches and the spirit in which they were given."

Pretty sharp preacher. In counseling we would say he reframed the event so it would appear more positive. So also when a man surrenders control of his life to God can he reframe even the most difficult events, knowing that his heavenly Father will use them for good in his life.

Let me insert something here. I've found that this step is the hardest for a man. He may admit, as David did in Psalm 40:12, "My sins have overtaken me." But he's so ashamed that he's not sure God will accept him or even wants to fix him. Do not confuse your heavenly Father with your earthly father or put the performance standards of society upon God.

If you have any doubt that God wants to fix you, just read Luke 15 and the parable of the prodigal son. The father in this story is representative of our heavenly Father, and this is the story of every man who realizes he can no longer do it on his own, is out of control and powerless, and has failed miserably. The text says, "But while he was still a long way off, his father saw him and was filled with compassion for him; he ran to his son, threw his arms around him and kissed him" (Luke 15:20).

God isn't the type of father who waits for us to come to him on our hands and knees to ask for something and then says, "Well, have you learned your lesson?" He doesn't even wait for us to get halfway to him before he meets us. No, he runs as fast as he can to us the first moment he sees any indication on our part that we have come to the realization that we need his help. God desperately wants to fix us—all we have to do is say, "Help me, Father."

3. I NEED TO TURN MY LIFE OVER TO GOD

Romans 12:1–2 says, "Therefore, I urge you, brothers, in view of God's mercy, to offer your bodies as living sacrifices, holy and pleasing to God—which is your spiritual act of worship. Do not conform any longer to the pattern of this world, but be transformed by the renewing of your mind. Then you will be able to test and approve what God's will is—his good, pleasing and perfect will." Notice that there are two key thoughts in these verses:

I decide to turn my life over to God because of his *goodness and mercy.* In our church we have a saying: "God is good all the time—and all the time God is good." I can turn my life over to God because I know that God's plans for me are much better than my own. I decide to turn my life over to God because I can trust God to take care of me.

Larry Kreider, in his book *Bottom Line Faith*, says,

When King David declared, "Many, O Lord, are the wonders you have done. The things you planned for us no one can recount to you; were I to speak and tell of them, they would be too many to declare" (Psalm 40:5), he didn't say everything we experience is delightful. But he assumes that God is good and all experiences weave a tapestry that, beyond any individual dreams, is more wonderful than we could imagine. Although the backside of that tapestry reveals a tangle of gnarled knots and twisted threads, the front side ultimately will reveal how meaningful each life experience can be for those who are yielded to Him.[1]

I need to turn my life over to God so I can renew my mind. If I'm going to have God's perspective, I must have his thoughts. Renewing my mind means that every issue I face as a man yielded to God comes under the microscope of Scripture. The first question that rolls off my lips is, "What would Jesus say and do in this situation?" Too often we men can get caught up in focusing on the urgent rather than in pursuing what's important. Our renewed mind determines where we put our emphasis.

A motivational speaker by the name of Jeff Conley sent me a series of questions he asks himself daily to make sure he keeps his mind renewed and focused on what's important. I've adapted them to fit me. They are:

1. Am I certain about what matters most?
2. Did I make a difference today?
3. Am I secure in who I am in Christ, regardless of my performance?
4. Did I schedule some quiet time today with the Lord?
5. Did I go out of my way to show my family that I love them?
6. Did I keep all my commitments? If not, why not?
7. Was I less than honest in any way today?
8. What did I learn today?
9. Was I kind to someone else without expecting anything in return?
10. Did I laugh today?
11. Did I work "heartily, as to the Lord" (Col. 3:23 KJV) today?
12. If today was a day off, did I rest or was I restless?
13. Did I emotionally support my loved ones by encouraging them, listening to them, and telling them that I love them?
14. What will I work on to be different tomorrow?
15. Did I live today in Rod's power or in God's power?

We must daily ask ourselves some hard questions so we keep our minds renewed and focused on God. My desire is that I wake up every morning with my mind on Jesus. If I renew my mind, I can truly "test and approve" what God's will is for me in any circumstance I encounter.

A friend of mine once said, "The only problem with a living sacrifice is that it wants to keep crawling off the altar." This passage in the book of Romans seems to indicate that the presenting of ourselves to God is a one-time offering, just like taking the vows at a wedding ceremony and saying, "Till death do us part." Yet, like marriage, we must make a conscious decision on a daily basis to remain faithful and realize that what we do today affects not only us but that other person as well. Admitting our need for God to be in control is a daily choice. It's something that needs to be done over and over, every time we feel tempted to take matters back into our own hands and to try to change our life through our own power.

I struggle with my need to admit my powerlessness, my need to let God fix me and to turn my life over to God. One of the ways I remind myself is through the lyrics of an old Scottish hymn. I call it my life hymn. The hymn is called "Be Thou My Vision." The lyrics say,

> Be Thou my vision, O Lord of my heart—
> Nought be all else to me, save that Thou art;
> Thou my best thought, by day or by night—
> Waking or sleeping, Thy presence my light.

> Be Thou my Wisdom, and Thou my true Word—
> I ever with Thee and Thou with me, Lord;
> Thou my great Father, I Thy true son—
> Thou in me dwelling, and I with Thee one.

> Riches I heed not, nor man's empty praise—
> Thou mine inheritance, now and always;
> Thou and Thou only, first in my heart—
> High King of heaven, my Treasure Thou art.

> High King of heaven, my victory won,
> May I reach heaven's joys, O bright heaven's Sun!
> Heart of my own heart, whatever befall,
> Still be my Vision, O Ruler of all.[2]

Maybe you haven't surrendered to him who wants you to experience life fully. Why not now? Before you go to the next chapter, admit that you are powerless and need him to manage your life. Admit that you need God to fix you and give you his perspective. Admit that you need him to take control of your life. You might want to pray the following:

*Lord, I'm desperate. I've hit the wall. I can't go on
living like this, feeling isolated from you and those I love.
I cry out, "Uncle!" Life has me in a bear hug and won't let
go. Please free me from this agony of never feeling that
enough is enough. Today I admit my need for you to be in
control. My need for you to fix me. My need for you to
manage my life. You said, "Come to me, all you who are
weary and burdened, and I will give you rest." I'm tired
and I seek your rest. Thank you for your offer. Today I'm
taking you up on it. Amen!*

DISCUSSION QUESTIONS

1.   On a scale of one to ten with ten being the most difficult, how
     difficult is it for you to admit to needing help from other men?
     What kind of messages keep you from believing that there are
     others who are willing to help you bear your burden?

2.   What kind of things can you do to trust god and depend on
     those he has sent to help you? What do you do to focus on
     Christ?

3.   Jesus was tempted with pride, to fulfill his purposes without
     trusting God and depending on others to help him. Who would
     have lost a blessing? Read Philippians 2:5–11 and Luke 8:1–3.

4.   What incidents can you recall that, given the perspective of
     time, have been reframed so you can see the good in them? Are
     you presently experiencing any such reframing? Read Romans
     8:28 and Jeremiah 29:11.

5.   Read Luke 15. What has the father been doing while the son is
     rebelling? Can you picture God waiting, watching and longing
     for you like that?

6.   Read through the list of questions on page 88. Use or modify
     this list for use in your small group or accountability group.

Chapter 6

In Process

It was a great day to play golf. The weather was perfect—sunny and eighty degrees. The setting was perfect—a beautifully manicured course in Hawaii. And the foursome was perfect—I was teeing off with a world-famous television personality.

Actually, I was just plain lucky to be paired with the celebrity. I arrived at the course by myself, so the starter put me with three other men. When it was time to tee up, I immediately recognized one of the guys. As an avid fan of ESPN's *Sportscenter,* I'm especially fond of John Saunders. Well, lo and behold, I was actually going to get to play golf with John (he told me to just call him John). Right away I was impressed with my golf companion. He was just as warm and outgoing in person as he seemed to be on TV.

When I stepped up to the ball to take my first shot, I was more than a little nervous. I was actually being watched by a world-famous sports announcer. I just kept telling myself, "Keep your eye on the ball and swing easy—the rest will take care of itself." And it did! Man, was I playing great. I was creaming the ball with my driver. I was lofting it with my wedge. I was tapping it softly with my putter. I half expected John to ask my why I wasn't on the tour. While he never did that, he did compliment me on my swing.

It was at the ninth hole that John discovered why I'm not on the tour. I really got a piece of the ball with my driver. Unfortunately, the piece was on one side of the ball, which sent it spinning horizontally. I sliced the ball so sharply, I wondered if it was a camouflaged boomerang. Once I blew that shot, I became self-conscious and my game self-destructed. By the time we reached the tenth hole, my game had dropped into the proverbial toilet. I mean, nothing went where I wanted it to go.

Amazingly, on the fifteenth hole everything turned around again. I landed a couple of pars and finished the round with a remnant of dignity. But overall I left the course feeling pretty low. I questioned if I'd ever play golf decently. And I couldn't help but wonder what John thought of me. I remember asking myself why I had to pay so much money just to get depressed.

However, I remembered watching Jack Nicholas play in the British Open. I consider Nicholas to be the greatest golfer of all time. Yet in the British Open, he hit his ball into a bunker and then took *four* shots to get out. In fact, he scored a ten on that hole. Imagine that—Jack Nicholas got a ten. I felt sorry for Nicholas but was comforted by the realization that history's greatest golfer had a bad day. I suspect he has lots of bad days.

Since that realization, I've enjoyed golf a lot more. Why? Because I understand that learning the game of golf is a process, one that never ends no matter how skilled someone may be. As long as I keep playing and practicing, I'll gradually improve.

I tell that story because I know a lot of men who have the same kind of frustration with their spiritual life. Just about the time they think they've got a handle on the game of life, they blow it. They make some sort of crazy decision or do something really destructive and sinful. At that moment, they feel like tossing the whole idea of the Christian life into the lake. It just seems too tough. Progress seems impossible.

As believers, we need to realize that our spiritual life is a lot like the game of golf—it's a process. It takes time. If we'll hang in there, by the grace of God we'll grow. We'll see changes.

In the last chapter, we looked at three of the Eight Steps to Building Brotherhood. We examined the first three steps we need to take to come out of isolation and develop shoulder-to-shoulder relationships. In this chapter, we're going to look at the five steps that make up the rest of the process.

4. I NEED TO MAKE A SEARCHING AND FEARLESS INVENTORY OF MYSELF

I'm absolutely convinced that the process of growth rests on our dedication to truth. Take, for example, a map. If I wanted to drive from Denver to Seattle, I know I'd have to travel in a westerly direction. But getting to Seattle in a reasonable period of time would require more than just following the setting sun. I'd need a map. If the map I used was forty years old, it probably wouldn't do me much good. At the time it was drawn, that map represented reality. But reality changes as new roads are built. And maps need to be updated so they represent those changes. I'd need an up-to-date map that accurately portrayed current roads, distances, and cities.

Of course, examining road maps, which represent the world outside, is never as painful as examining the world within. Yet if we're going to progress in our relationship with God and other people, we must be totally dedicated to the truth. And our dedication should drive us to make an accurate map of ourselves, one that reflects our fears, disappointments, addictions, sins, resentments, strengths, weaknesses, and other things we would rather keep hidden—things we would rather not face the truth about.

The temptation at this stage is to lie to ourselves, to white-wash reality so we don't look all that bad. So we don't have to experience the pain of seeing our flaws. So we don't have to suffer the pain of letting go of some attitudes and actions we've been holding on to. But you can't do that. You need a map of yourself that reflects reality so you can move on with the growth process. Taking this step requires courage. It demands fearlessness. And it necessitates an infusion of the grace of God.

Every time I go through this process myself or encourage other men to do so, I'm reminded of the woman Jesus spoke with at the well. Understandably, she tried to cover up some of the facts of her life. She didn't want this young rabbi to know she'd been married five times and was living with a man to whom she wasn't married. Those weren't the kinds of things she liked to think about or talk about. Yet Jesus exposed this reality. He made it clear he knew all about her. He let her know he'd read the entire map of her life. And then he loved and accepted her in the face of this reality. His expression of acceptance transformed her life (John 4:1–42).

As you take this step, meditate on the words of Psalm 139:23–24: "Search me, O God, and know my heart; test me and know my anxious thoughts. See if there is any offensive way in me, and lead me in the way everlasting." Because you've turned your life over to God, you have the assurance that he'll give you the insight you need to unearth those things that are hidden in the recesses of your memory. But more than that, God will accept you.

To help you take this crucial step, I've devised a plan for you to follow. Tell your story by writing in a journal the central events and experiences of your life:

1. *List all the addictive processes and substances in your life now or in the past.* You might want to look back over chapter 2 to help you with this. Try to trace the roots of your addictions by examining your family of origin

and noting how experiences in your formative years may have contributed.

2. *Make an inventory of major relationships in your life. List the important people in your past and present.* Describe the relationships from the perspective of your feelings. Look for unhealthy and painful patterns that have reappeared. Look for guilt feelings related to people in the above list. Remember, there's a difference between "real" and "false" guilt. You might feel guilty because your son didn't excel in athletics. But in reality he suffered a serious knee injury while playing high school football, not because of anything you did. I would identify such feelings as false guilt. If, on the other hand, you failed to attend any of his practices or games and ridiculed his play, your feelings stem from real guilt. Since in step 5 you'll acknowledge and confess any real harm you've done to others, it's crucial for you to identify all legitimate guilt in your life.

3. *Make a list of all the good things in your life.* You'll want to identify the positive legacies you received from childhood, healthy survival skills you've learned, talents, abilities, and positive steps you've taken to grow as an individual.

4. *Develop a list of all your resentments.* This is a crucial step. Men can sometimes stuff their anger. Over time it turns into resentment and rage. When I lived in Oregon, I remember reading about the problems they were having with the waste material from the nuclear reactor on the Columbia River. While they could put it into drums and bury it, eventually the nuclear waste would destroy the drums and pollute the soil and poison the groundwater. Resentment's like that. It has to be dealt with properly or it'll destroy you.

When you take this step, be sure to identify the underlying causes of the resentment. See if you can figure out what unmet need triggered the anger and later resentment. It may be that you feared a loss of financial security or relational intimacy.

The primary reason for identifying your resentments is so you can grieve your old unmet needs. A number of years ago while serving in a church, I felt a need for both financial and relational affirmation. After years of fruitful work there, I felt God directing me to another ministry. Rather than affirming my ministry and making the transition easy, the church cut me off financially and wished me good luck. My need for appreciation and financial security wasn't met, and it caused real anger and resentment. It took me years to embrace and grieve that unmet need. Until I could work through that resentment, I viewed other people in similar settings through the lens of my pain.

As you inventory your resentments, complete the following statements:

I have resented _____

I was angry because _____

I was hurt because _____

My hurt stemmed from the fear that _____

_____

The need that was unmet was _____

_____1

As I watched the movie *The Shawshank Redemption,* I couldn't help but draw some parallels between the experience of Andy DuFresne and men who take the fourth step. In the movie, DuFresne is wrongly convicted for the murder of his unfaithful wife and her lover, Giv. He's sent to Shawshank, a maximum-security prison run by brutish guards and a hypocritical, Bible-quoting warden. Veteran convict "Red" Redding, with his bassetlike sad eyes, soon recognizes something different about DuFresne. The new kid's aloof. He lacks the edge, that gallows swagger and humor.

It doesn't take long for DuFresne, a soft-spoken banker, to make a name for himself by using his business skills. In a short time he's in demand as a tax preparer and financial adviser to the prison guards. But life in prison is one of oppression and hopelessness. Eventually Andy decides to escape. Slowly, night after night, he digs a tunnel. Because he knows the process will take years, he's not in a hurry. In fact, he excavates so slowly that nobody notices what's happening—including the audience. Finally, in an amazing scene, he squeezes through the tiny passageway and then crawls through a five-hundred-foot-long sewage pipe. On the other side, he stands free in the open night air. He finds redemption from a life of misery.

Likewise, every man must decide he's had enough of the isolation and misery. He must decide to make the painful inventory, even though at times he may feel as if he's crawling through a sewage pipe. On the other side there's life and hope. Remember that as you make your inventory. The process takes time and may be painful. But it's worth it. Just ask Andy DuFresne.

5. I Must Admit to God and Another Person the Exact Nature of My Wrongs

Once you've completed your personal inventory, you're ready for the next step—telling God and another man everything you've done wrong. I have to tell you, this is a tough one. It involves connecting at a deep, personal level with another man. It means letting down your guard. It means doing the one thing you've been programmed all your life *not* to do. It's the opposite of running and hiding. It's stopping and confessing.

Take a look at 2 Samuel 12:1–13. There's probably no better example of this step than what King David did here. Having committed adultery and murder, he had run from God for over a year. During that time he'd refused to take responsibility for his actions. Perhaps he figured he'd behaved no worse than other kings of his day.

Finally he was confronted by Nathan. The prophet approached David and asked him to give a ruling on a civil case. The crime involved two neighbors. One had a vast herd of sheep. The other had a single pet lamb. When a friend visited the wealthy man, he could've slaughtered any of the animals from his flock and served it to his guest. Instead, he stole his neighbor's pet lamb, killed it, and cooked it.

Upon hearing this story, David exploded with anger and said, "As surely as the LORD lives, the man who did this deserves to die!" (v. 5).

Nathan lifted a finger in the king's face and said, "You are the man!" (v. 7).

David could have denied his guilt. He could have rationalized. Instead, he said, "I have sinned against the LORD" (v. 13).

The king probably thought he'd rendered his own death sentence. Instead, Nathan said, "The LORD has taken away your sin. You are not going to die" (v. 13).

Slowly the prophet turned and left. The guards, statesmen, and servants left. As the great cedar doors closed, David sat alone. With tears streaming down his cheeks and dripping onto his royal robe, he reached for his scroll and a writing tool. There upon his throne, alone with God, he penned Psalm 32.

As David reflected on what had just happened, he overflowed with happiness. Forgiveness was what he needed and forgiveness was what he found. He expressed his joy when he wrote, "Blessed is he whose transgressions are forgiven, whose sins are covered" (Ps. 32:1). Like David, you need to acknowledge your sin to God and to another man. While seeking forgiveness is tough, the reward of a clear conscience is worth it. To help you do this, let's examine the process David went through.

Uncover It

When David wrote, "I acknowledged my sin" (Ps. 32:5), the word for "acknowledged" meant "to make known." Obviously, God knew about David's sin all along—just as he knows about ours. But God wants us to own our sins. We do that when we admit our wrongdoing to him and another person.

We all know what it's like to hide, to cover up our wrongdoing so others don't see it. David tried that tactic. On the day he found forgiveness, he wrote, "I uncovered my sin . . . I exposed it." There's something profound about David's statement. In verse 1 we find that God covered David's sin when he admitted it. The verb for "cover" is a different form of the same verb found in verse 5 for "uncover." When we try to hide our sins so God won't see them, they remain visible. But when we expose our wrongdoing to God, he hides them.

Do you see what that means? If you're trying to hide your sin, you won't succeed. But when you uncover your sins, God will hide them.

A Safe Place to Hide

The natural outgrowth of forgiveness is worship. No longer did David see God as someone to hide from. Instead, God became his hiding place. David couldn't protect himself from guilt and shame. But God could. David couldn't guard himself from the destructive power of sin. But God could.

We saw in chapter 1 that as fallen men, we spend most of our lives hiding from God and each other. When we take the fifth step, we're no longer hiding from God, we're running to him. We're allowing him to be our hiding place.

Admitting our sins to God prepares us to admit them to another person. Once God has forgiven us, we go in his power to the individual we believe is best-suited to hear our confession.

Rehearse What You'll Say

In the story of the prodigal son, the son rehearsed in detail what he would say to his father upon his return. He'd committed great sins against his father. And he felt deep remorse. He wasn't expecting unconditional forgiveness. He just hoped his father would accept his confession and restore him to any position.

As you consider the wrongs you've committed, write them down. Identify someone you trust (a pastor, close friend, or counselor) and let them know why you want to meet with them. Rehearse what you're going to say and then say it.

Your admission of guilt doesn't shift the blame onto anybody else. You're not minimizing what you've done wrong. You're owning your sin.

This is a very difficult step, but it's crucial. And it leads to the next one.

6. I WILL ASK GOD TO REMOVE MY DEFECTS

I suspect you'll read this chapter in a single setting, or two at the most. Once you've read the chapter, it'll take time to go through each step. By the time you get to this step, you should have your personal inventory completed. And it should give you insight into the defects in your character and behavior. Since you've admitted your sins to another person, you now need to ask God to remove these shortcomings in your life. It's not enough to simply admit that the problems exist; you need to begin the process of change.

As I think about the importance of this step, I'm reminded of the story of the man who was driving his pickup along a farm road in eastern Oklahoma. He hadn't been driving long when he caught up with an eighteen-wheeler. After he'd followed the truck for about five miles, the driver pulled the huge rig over to the side of the road and climbed out of the cab. Thinking maybe the driver had a problem, the man in the pickup also pulled over. He was shocked when the truck driver climbed out of the cab holding a baseball bat, which he used to pound on the sides of the trailer. After he'd circled the entire trailer, the driver got back in the cab and started up again.

Every five miles for the next twenty miles, the truck driver repeated that strange procedure. When they finally reached a town, the truck driver pulled his rig into the parking lot of a truck stop. The man in the pickup approached the truck driver and said, "I've been following you for the last twenty-five miles, and I was wondering why you stop every five miles and pound on the sides of your trailer with a baseball bat."

The truck driver smiled and said, "Well, you see, I got a twenty-thousand-pound rig, and I'm carrying twenty-five thousand pounds of canaries. To keep my rig from getting stuck, I have to keep five thousand pounds of canaries in the air at all times."

Sometimes we're like that driver. We have all kinds of things going on in our life that can cause us to get stuck. Instead of dealing with the problem at its root, we approach it on a short-term, superficial basis. Step 6 requires us to ask ourselves, "What's going on in my life that causes me to get stuck? What do I need God to transform?" The key to this step is a willingness to have God remove *all* character defects.

Identify those areas of your life in which you know you tend to get stuck, areas that you know are out of balance. You may identify a lust problem. Maybe it'll be a struggle with money, anger, substance abuse, workaholism, or overeating.

Once you've tagged an area of your life, tell God you know you can't overcome this character defect on your own. Ask him to touch this part of your life and heal you. Be willing to undergo discomfort while the change is taking place. Making the change won't feel normal. But God can transform you.

I once heard a story about two caterpillars who were traveling across a field one day when the shadow of a butterfly passed over them. As the two looked up at the beautiful creature, one said to the other, "Man, you'd never get me to fly in one of those things!" You're like that caterpillar—God's in the process of transforming you. The process may seem a bit unnatural at times, but the change is what you need to seek and pray for.

Follow the example of King David. After confessing his sins, he prayed, "Create in me a pure heart, O God, and renew a steadfast spirit within me" (Ps. 51:10). He knew that only God could change him. For God to change you, you need to be willing to ask him to do whatever it takes. And I'll guarantee you, God can and will change you. He's changed me. And I've seen him change countless other men. But it begins by asking him to make those changes.

7. I WILL RIGHT AS MANY WRONGS AS I CAN

In the previous three steps, we examined our defects, admitted them to God and another person, and asked God to transform us. Now our focus changes. In the final two steps, we begin the process of rebuilding our relationship with other people and with God.

You need to take a long, hard look at the way you've treated other people throughout your life. That's exactly what Zacchaeus did. The Jewish tax collector was hated by everybody in Jericho.

He collected taxes for the Romans, who allowed him to skim off the top any extra money he could collect. And he probably collected plenty of extra money. Once he came to faith in Christ, he said, "If I have cheated anybody out of anything, I will pay back four times the amount" (Luke 19:8).

That's the attitude we all should ask God to give us. To help you do that, take some time and identify everyone you've harmed or think you've harmed, dead or alive, living next door or around the world. At this point don't get hung up on whether or not you can make amends. Just make as exhaustive a list as you can. You might use the following as a guideline:

Those I Harmed   *How I Harmed Them*

_____   _____

_____   _____

_____   _____

_____   _____

_____   _____

_____   _____

_____   _____

_____   _____

_____   _____

Obviously, you need to identify people you've physically or verbally harmed. But there are others ways you may have harmed others. You may have hurt someone by being overly possessive or controlling. Perhaps you've consistently played the role of a martyr or victim. Maybe you've been too rigid. It could be that you've failed to honestly express your feelings in a loving way.

Once you've completed this list, ask God to show you those people you need to seek out so you can ask for their forgiveness and possibly make restitution. Before meeting with them or talking with them on the phone, be sure to rehearse what you'll say to them. I'd suggest something like this: "God has shown me that I've sinned against you by _____. I'm deeply sorry. Will you forgive me?"

I'll never forget hearing Bill McCartney, the founder of Promise Keepers, tell the story at a P.K. rally about a man who had stolen thirty thousand dollars from his business partner. After reconnecting with God and other men, he returned home and paid back the money. A friend of mine met with a college professor and admitted cheating on an exam two years before. One man asked his children to forgive him for not affirming them.

Be careful that you don't set unrealistic expectations for these meetings. There's no guarantee that just because you meet with someone and ask for their forgiveness, the relationship will be healed. Your purpose is to do all you can to promote healing. As much as you're able, you're to be at peace with everyone (Rom. 12:18). Ask God for the grace you need to take every step you can to make amends for the hurt you've caused others.

8. I WILL SEEK TO GROW SPIRITUALLY THROUGH PRAYER AND BIBLE STUDY

Each of the seven steps you've taken so far prepares the way for this final step. Actually, this isn't a step but a process. More than anything else, God wants a relationship with you. Just as he pursued Adam in the garden, so he pursues you. Spiritual growth demands that you slow down enough to cultivate your relationship with God.

Early on, you may feel unworthy to approach God. Every time you're plagued with those feelings, remember that Jesus has taken away your guilt and shame. He paid for your sins, and there's no need for you to punish yourself with guilt. Paul declared that there's "no condemnation for those who are in Christ Jesus" (Rom. 8:1).

When you talk with God, don't feel you have to communicate with some sort of religious jargon. Talk to God openly and honestly. Express your feelings, fears, and joys. I'd urge you to keep a spiritual journal and jot down some of your prayers—along with God's answers. Try to set aside some time every day, even if it's only a few minutes, to read the Bible. As you read it, if something jumps out at you, write that down in your journal.

Remember, spiritual growth is a process. As you grow in your relationship with God, you'll discover that your relationships with other men will also grow. In fact, you'll find that your relationships with other men will help you grow spiritually.

I opened this chapter by talking about golf. The truth is, I can't help but think about my golf game whenever I consider the spiritual process we're all involved in. When I first started playing golf, I was a graduate student working on my Ph.D. Man, was I ever a hacker. But I loved the game, so I kept practicing and playing. Over the years I slowly improved. Nowadays I actually have more good shots than bad ones, more low scores than high ones. But I sure haven't arrived. So I just keep practicing and playing.

That's what we all need to do spiritually. We need to keep practicing and playing and enjoying God, our friends, and life. As we do that, we'll discover we're growing deeper spiritually and relationally. We'll find that we're actually drawn to close friendships with other men—friendships that provide us safety and encouragement, friendships that make us feel that we're part of a team.

DISCUSSION QUESTIONS

1. Dr. Cooper tells the story of the woman at the well in John 4. Reread that story. Make note of the woman's defense mechanisms. As you proceed with the writing exercises in this chapter, imagine that you are that woman and that Jesus is the one who has begun the conversation with you. It is his love of you that longs for and makes possible your transformation.

2. As a group read through the Scripture verses listed in this chapter. Discuss over the next few weeks where each man is in the process of taking inventory.

CHAPTER 7

The Huddle

I used to be the chaplain for the Houston Oilers when Earl Campbell played for them and they were in their heyday. The players at that time often talked about their desire to have a "no-cut contract." This contract would guarantee that if they ever got hurt, they would continue to be paid and would not be cut from the team.

Mike, a buddy of mine who played linebacker, was a hunk, to put it bluntly. He was six three, weighed 235 pounds, was tall, dark, handsome, and all muscle. He was good—but not good enough. He got cut from the team. When he told me, he asked me something that floored me. Mike said, "Rod, now that I'm no longer playing with the Oilers, will we still be friends?"

I was shocked. I said, "Sure, Mike. I like you, not because you play ball but because you are Mike." Man, was he ever relieved. You see, he was in an environment that said, "If you do not perform, you are out—both professionally and relationally."

I find that many men would like a no-cut contract. They would like to know that even when they are not performing their best or are hurt, they are still on the team and do not need to fear competition. But that's not how the world—and sad to say, at times the church as well—operates. Therefore many men continue to play hurt and stay isolated from one another. They stay in hiding because it's wrong to not at least appear to have it all together, especially spiritually.

After Mike had been out of football for a while, I asked him what he missed most about pro ball. I was surprised by his answer. He said it was when they got in the huddle on the field. I asked him why. He replied that in the huddle you felt safe. It was a place where you could come and get encouragement, direction, support, and correction. It was also a place where you could regroup for the next phase of the battle and know that you had ten other guys with you to help you win. Mike said it was especially nice to have the huddle when they were playing away-games in hostile stadiums, where it seemed they had to battle not only the team but also the negative environment. He said the huddle was a sanctuary—a place you could go back to for encouragement to keep going.

Like Mike, every man needs the huddle. He needs a safe place where he can go and get what he needs to enter into the next phase of life's conflict. If a man's going to survive—no, win—the battles of his life, he must have a huddle of good men around him to cheer him on and bandage his wounds in the midst of the fight. He needs to know that he has men around him who will celebrate with him in the good times and do whatever it takes to bring help and healing in the bad times. He needs the kind of buddies a certain man had in Mark 2:1–5.

Let me set the scene. Jesus had entered the small village of Capernaum, which was a kind of base of operations for him in the northern part of the country. It appears that Jesus went to a small house, possibly the house of Peter and Andrew (Mark 1:29). His presence in the little village was soon discovered, so Jesus had no privacy. The house began to fill with people, to the point that they were overflowing onto the porch and out into the street. The people were there to hear Jesus preach. I'm sure they also were there in the hope that Jesus might heal some of them from their diseases and other ailments. At least, that's what four men carrying a friend on a stretcher hoped:

> Some men came, bringing to him a paralytic, carried by four of them. Since they could not get him to Jesus because of the crowd, they made an opening in the roof above Jesus and, after digging through it, lowered the mat the paralyzed man was lying on. When Jesus saw their faith, he said to the paralytic, "Son, your sins are forgiven."
>
> Mark 2:3–5

To understand the commitment of these men to their friend, we need to understand what they were willing to do to help him. You see, the typical peasant's house in Palestine was usually a small, one-room structure with a flat roof accessible by means of an outside stairway. The roof itself was usually made of wooden beams, with thatch and compacted earth to shed the rain. Sometimes tiles were laid between the beams and the thatch. These men went and got their friend to bring him to Jesus. When they saw the size of the crowd, they realized it was impossible to enter by the door. So they carried their friend on his stretcher up the outside stairway to the roof, began ripping up the compacted thatch and earth with their bare hands, removed the tiles, and then lowered the man through the now-exposed beams to the floor below.

Can you imagine the shocked look on Jesus' face when all of a sudden he hears this ripping overhead, watches debris falling everywhere, and then sees this man being lowered right down in front of him? And how about the man on the stretcher? Capernaum was a small village, so perhaps there were those in the crowd who knew him. I can see him being lowered, and on the way down saying, "Hello, John.... How you doing, Mary?" What a scene. Jesus was so impressed that he not only healed the man physically (Mark 2:11–12) but also healed him internally. Why? Please do not miss this phrase: "Jesus saw their faith."

This man had a huddle. Look at three things his friends did for him:

1. *They went and got him.* Isn't that what we need and want from our friends? They were so committed to their friend that they pursued him and looked out for his well-being. They were there for him. Every man needs that kind of commitment from his friends.

2. *They did whatever it took to meet his need.* Notice that they worked as a team and tore up that roof to get him help. Every man needs a team that'll help him remove the obstacles in his life so he might get healed. We all have been paralyzed in some area and need the help of our huddle to bring healing to us and remove obstacles that would prevent such healing.

3. *They brought him to Jesus.* They knew Jesus had the ability to bring healing to their friend. They had faith. Every man needs men who have faith in him and in Jesus. Men need men around who will bring them to Jesus when they can't get there themselves, so true healing can take place in their lives.

Wow! What a huddle. Do you have a huddle like that in your life? Would you like to? Good. But what does it take to have a successful huddle? What type of relational environment must the huddle have to sustain a man, and even transform him into Christlikeness, when he faces the problems and perplexities of life? Well, let's look at the ultimate Coach and his huddle of men. You know who I'm talking about—none other than Jesus and his disciples.

CONFORM OR TRANSFORM?

I've found that there's usually one of two types of relational climates in most men's huddle groups. One will sustain a man, and the other will sink him spiritually. One relational climate is called the transformational environment, and the other is called the conformity environment. There are several traits consistent with a man who is in a conformity environment:

In relationships this man

Feels he has to be good or perfect to be loved

Fears expressing emotions—especially anger

Has difficulty trusting others

This man's moods are characterized by

Frequent sadness, anxiety, and perhaps emptiness

Inner feelings of frustration, anger, and dissatisfaction

His spiritual state consists of

An inability to feel better in spite of spiritual effort, prayer, and Bible study

Feeling more afraid of God than loved by him

A pervasive sense of guilt, even about small, unimportant things

Difficulty enjoying life, because it's somehow unspiritual to enjoy it

A checklist mentality—he tries to follow a list of rules to be spiritual

These characteristics most likely describe a good number of men in today's men's ministries and especially in so-called accountability groups. Wellington Boone, a national speaker for Promise Keepers, put it well when he said, "Accountability groups are not merely for sin management but should help a man grow into the image of Jesus Christ." Right on, Wellington.

The huddle should be a place where a man doesn't just keep a set of rules and get hammered when he breaks them. The huddle is where he can go and admit his weakness and have a team help him grow through that weakness into Christlikeness.

So what kind of environment did Jesus provide for his huddle? I mean, if there was any group that was constantly not measuring up, it was his disciples. What kind of relational climate did Jesus create to bring out the best in his men? I believe it was the transformational environment. Let's look at the four characteristics of the transformational environment and compare them with those of the conformity environment.

An Atmosphere of Acceptance and Security

There's a religious group in the New Testament that loved to keep the rules. The Pharisees operated from the conformity environment model. Rigid rules? You bet!

One clash between Jesus and the Pharisees occurred in Matthew 12:1–8. Jesus and his disciples were walking through the grainfields. They were hungry and began picking the heads of grain. Oh, yeah—it was on the Sabbath. By picking the heads of grain, the disciples were harvesting. By rubbing them between their hands before eating them, they were threshing. That was against the rules, according to the Pharisees. But look at Jesus' response to this complaint. He reminded them of the Scripture that says, "I desire mercy, not sacrifice" (Matt. 12:7). Jesus knew that the rules were made for man, not man for the rules. God's law creates an environment that accepts a man where he is and helps him get where he needs to be. The focus is on the needs of the man.

There's also a sense of security—especially when a man makes a mistake. Have you ever played Nintendo? That's the conformity environment if there ever was one. You have certain rules and you'd better follow them. If you don't, you're punished. You may lose points, you may lose a "life." Lose enough lives and you're done—game over.

The Pharisees would've loved it. They once brought to Jesus a woman who had been caught in the act of adultery. What they were doing there is another story, but suffice it to say that she was found out. They wanted Jesus to condemn her. After all, she'd been caught in a sin deserving death—game over.

Jesus turned the tables. He asked them to examine their hearts before condemning her. He told her that he didn't condemn her and commanded her to go and sin no more. He offered a redemptive solution.

Notice that Jesus didn't overlook her sin but first of all made it clear that there's no such thing as spiritual superiority. When he said to the Pharisees, "If any one of you is without sin, let him be the first to throw a stone at her" (John 8:7), he leveled the playing field. A conformity huddle has the attitude, "There go I but by the grace of God." A man can feel secure in knowing he can share his guts and the team will not pick up stones to throw at him—but will be there to help him "sin no more."

The focus of the Pharisees was on conformity. Luke 11 tells us what was important to them. They cleaned the outside of the cup and didn't care what was inside. They tithed even down to the smallest seed from their gardens—and made sure everyone knew it—but they neglected God's larger law of justice and love of him. Jesus said in the Sermon on the Mount that when they prayed, they prayed loud and long so everyone would hear. But according to Jesus, what was important was the inside of a man. It was the substance of his prayers.

Jesus provided his disciples with an environment of acceptance and security. He related to his men in a way that called for transformation, not conformity. Let's see how these two environments match up so far:

Conformity	*Transformational*
Adheres to rigid rules	Empowered by rules
Punishes wrongdoing	Focuses on redemptive solutions
Appearance is all-important	Substance is all-important

An Atmosphere of Openness

Emotional openness. I have a picture of a laughing Jesus. One of my clients gave it to me. Jesus has a big grin and is in the middle of a big belly laugh. Children loved being with Jesus. He was even accused of partying too much. Why? Because he made people feel safe and therefore they could be open with him.

The emotional climate of the Pharisees was a tense one. There were so many rules, so many laws. If you broke any of them, you were unclean. The question the disciples asked about the man born blind reflects how the culture of that day viewed disabilities. Was it his sin or his parents' sin? It was a blaming, judgmental time. Jesus' response put it into perspective. It was neither; it was done for the glory of God (John 9:1–3). His response reached out to the man and gave him safety, acceptance, and care. Jesus ate with sinners and tax collectors. He let prostitutes minister to him. He touched lepers. People who came into contact with Jesus were allowed to be themselves. No pretense, no faking. Just share who you are.

Every man needs that type of huddle. A place where he can go and just be himself. Where he can voice his frustrations, fears, and failures and know they will not be used against him. If you want to keep a man stuck, don't let him be emotional. It's in the huddle where he needs to feel that he can let it out and then process it.

Intellectual openness. Did you ever notice that there were no dumb questions with Jesus? In fact, he invited questions and open discussion. James and John asked for the seats on his right and his left in glory. Jesus didn't rebuke them for asking. Peter asked, "What do we get for following you?" To us, it sounds like a selfish, rude question. But Jesus answered him. Now don't get me wrong. Jesus did hold his disciples accountable. For instance, when Peter chastised Christ for talking about his death, Jesus told Peter in no uncertain terms to quit buying into Satan's agenda. There's accountability but it's couched in love.

In a conformity system, values are rigidly held and contrary views unacceptable. But there were no untouchable areas with Jesus. In the Sermon on the Mount he talked about sex, money, adultery, divorce. He talked politics and many times talked about his own death.

And this "no untouchable areas" ideal didn't remain just talk. It permeated his life. Have you ever heard of the "black-and-blue Pharisees"? The Pharisees weren't allowed to talk to women. Women were culturally unacceptable. So these Pharisees would close their eyes and run into a wall. In contrast, Jesus started a conversation with the woman at the well, despite the fact that she was also a Samaritan and the Jews hated Samaritans. He spoke to her and offered her living water.

The huddle needs to allow a man the ability to bring up tough issues so he can work through them. Healing comes about by allowing a man to get the secrets out of his life. If the huddle does not allow a man emotional and intellectual openness, he'll never progress along the path to healing and Christlikeness.

In terms of openness, let's compare the two environments:

Conformity	*Transformational*
Tense, tight, defensive	Comfortable, safe, trusting
Blaming and judgmental	Spontaneous, accepting, caring
Contrary views unacceptable	No untouchable areas, free and wide-ranging discussions

An Atmosphere of Team

All for one and one for all. Two stories in the Bible represent Jesus' approach to teamwork. In Luke 10, Jesus sent out the seventy-two to minister. He gave them instructions and turned them loose. And they were successful. Did Jesus become threatened by their success? Did he feel they were stealing the limelight? No. The Bible says he rejoiced greatly.

He sent his disciples out again after he'd risen from the dead. Matthew notes that some were doubtful as to his presence. So he comforted them, giving them authority. How many of you have been in a position of having responsibility but not authority? It's not a good way to try to get work done. But Jesus gives his followers the authority and shares the responsibility. And he promises his presence throughout the process.

Every man wants to know that he has the support of his huddle. A man doesn't mind being confronted with the truth when he knows that those who confront him will be with him when he has to make painful changes and face reality. Confrontation without commitment leads to destruction.

I was told the story of a man who had committed adultery and knew he needed to tell his wife. He was scared, certain that when he told her, there would be incredible pain and disruption in his family. He told his huddle, and every one of them began to weep with him, knowing that they also could be in the same position. They agreed that he needed to tell his wife. When it was time for him to share this painful news with her, they went as a group and shared in the responsibility of helping him as their teammate, and them as a couple, begin the process of healing. The wife was devastated, but her husband's knowledge that these men were going to be there in the restoration process helped salvage that marriage and restore that brother to the kingdom. One for all—and all for one.

In summary:

Conformity	*Transformational*
"Just do it" mind-set	Team oriented—"we can do it" mind-set

An Atmosphere of Loving Accountability and Growth

I've found that in a transformational environment, love is unconditional. In a conformity environment, love is conditional on behavior. You could be in one week and out the next. Let me show you what I mean:

Conformity	*Transformational*
Controlling. Maintains lists of shoulds and should nots. Focuses on behavior.	Develops spiritual disciplines. Relational. Encourages the brother to question, think, express, and work with his feelings and become aware and responsible. Focuses on process.
Punishes wrongdoing. Relationships stay surface-level and task-driven.	Guides, confronts, and encourages. Believes the best for the brother. Relationships are warm, relaxed, trusting, and mutually respecting.

I've had the opportunity to be in both types of huddles. The one (guess which), I left feeling beat-up, never quite adequate, and often alone in the process. The other, I left encouraged, convicted, and hopeful I could do what was needed, because these men were squarely behind me, urging me on in Christlikeness.

I have a huddle that I meet with on Wednesday mornings. These men are my lifeline. I'll never forget when I came to my group and shared the frustrations concerning my communication with my wife, Nancy. They began to lovingly probe me and pointed out that I was traveling over half the time. They also pointed out that communication was tough because I would "veg out" at home and not take the time to talk. I defended myself, but they put the ball squarely back into my court. They said, "Rod, you didn't make the vow 'Till death do us part' to Promise Keepers, but you did to Nancy. Don't you think it's time to change?" They were right. They've helped me take time out with Nancy, as well as showed me how to cut back on my schedule to stay home more—to be a Promise Keeper. They didn't let up on me, but at the same time they helped me in the process. These men hold me accountable, but they do it not by shaking fingers at me but by locking arms with me.

If you want to see the result of being in a transformational environment, look at the disciples after the Resurrection. They went from being fearful followers with little faith to being national leaders, the foundation of the church. Peter cowered in an upper room and then preached before crowds, getting arrested in the process. Did this change result from conformity to a set of rules? No, Peter had been transformed by Jesus.

Look at John 21. Peter had denied Christ three times. He was now out fishing, because that at least was something he could do. They had been hard at it with no success. Peter saw someone on the shore telling them where to throw their nets. The stranger said, "Throw your net on the right side of the boat and you will find some" (v. 6). And they did, so much so that the nets began to break. All of a sudden the feeling came over Peter that this had happened before, and he knew he was in the presence of Jesus. He was naked, meaning he was unacceptable in his present state to be before God. So he did the only rational thing he could do—he covered himself, jumped into the water, and headed for shore.

This next part is special. How did Jesus confront Peter? Did he make him conform to a standard, shake his finger at him in rage, belittle him, or tell him that he just didn't measure up? No. Jesus first made breakfast for Peter. Eating a meal together demonstrated fellowship. And then Jesus asked the most penetrating question: "Do you love me?" You know the story. Three times Jesus asked Peter, "Do you love me?" Then he restored Peter to a strategic position in front of his peers. Jesus let Peter know that just because he failed, it didn't mean he was a failure. He could start fresh. Failing doesn't mean that you are out of the game. Jesus gave his men freedom to fail.

Here's what a man from a transformational environment looks like:

In relationships this man

Recognizes that he's secure in his relationship with Christ

Has the ability to set appropriate limits

Has clear lines of communication with his family and encourages their growth

Expresses his emotions appropriately, especially anger

Is trustworthy and trusting

This man's moods are characterized by

A general state of fulfillment and contentment

His spiritual state consists of

Trusting in the character of God, whether emotionally up or down

Deeply loving God and feeling loved by him

Appropriate guilt

Enjoying life and living by biblical principles

Jesus said, "Come to me, all you who are weary and burdened, and I will give you rest" (Matt. 11:28). We might paraphrase it to state, "Come to me, all who are tired of the game, all who have fumbled, all who are bruised and broken, and I will give you a place to huddle." If a man's going to know Christ deeply and keep his promises, he must know that the huddle he comes to is a place of rest and safety.

A friend of mine has a creed he follows with his shoulder-to-shoulder partners:

> I owe you my loyalty, even to my heart, but I do not owe you my agreement on everything.
> I owe you tolerance and encouragement and recognition of your gift.
> I owe you part of me—my time, my thought, my possessions, and my vulnerability.
> I owe you serious consideration of your admonishment of me.
> I owe you my forgiveness—a friend who truly forgives does not need to forget.

This is the kind of man I feel safe with—and one who will help transform my life into Christlikeness.

I believe that if a man's going to be accountable, he must have this type of relational environment from his teammates. Yet the word "accountability" is something men shy away from with each other. If accountability is central to pursuing godliness, what keeps us from seeking it? The conformity environment may be a part of it, but there are some others. In the next chapter, we'll look at some of the key barriers that stop us from being accountable and developing deep shoulder-to-shoulder relationships with our brothers.

DISCUSSION QUESTIONS

1. Are you willing to be the kind of friend and take the kind of risks that is described in Mark 2:1–5? Why or why not? What steps can you take to accomplish this?

2. Read Luke 15. What kind of system, conformity or transformational, brought about the change in the younger son? From what system did the elder son operate? Give reasons for your answers. What was the father offering to his sons?

3. Dr. Cooper discusses Luke 11 on page 113. Identify the various ways the Pharisees tried to stay hidden. (Refer back to chapter 1 if necessary.)

4. What would it mean to you to have Jesus accept you just as you are, no pretense, no faking? What would it mean to you to have a group of men accept you just as you are, no pretense, no faking?

5. "A man doesn't mind being confronted with the truth when he knows that those who confront him will be with him when he has to make painful changes and face reality. Confrontation without _____ leads to destruction." Compare this statement with Ephesians 4:25, 31–32.

6. Read Luke 22:32. What priestly function does Jesus perform, even knowing Peter will deny him? Read John 21:1–17. What priestly function does Christ perform here? What impact does it have on you to know that Christ is interceding for you even in your sins, and that he stands ready to restore you to himself when you turn again?

PART THREE

Strategies for Achieving Brotherhood

8. Breaking Through Relational Barriers

The first step in developing accountability involves identifying the reasons men give for not wanting to be held accountable. Such thoughts as "I might lose face" or "I might fail" have to be brought into the light. Each barrier must be broken, and relational bridges constructed in their place. These relational bridges make for an accountable relationship of openness and trust.

9. What Works for You

Fundamental to benefiting from a relationship of accountability is understanding your personality style. This chapter will describe four basic personality styles, how they respond to accountability, and the relational atmosphere necessary to maintain accountability. The chapter will show the reader what he needs according to his temperament, and how he should respond to other men according to their temperament.

10. Accountability and the Stages of Man's Life

Each stage of a man's life brings with it unique issues. There are various difficulties a man encounters as he transitions from one stage of life to another. This chapter will identify the issues a man needs to be accountable for in each stage of life, so he can successfully make the transition. It'll also help him identify the issues other men need to address, according to where they are in life.

11. The Blessings of Brotherhood

This chapter will describe the benefits of an accountable relationship, such as support in times of need, unconditional acceptance, and courage to change. All this occurs in a setting in which each man is striving to become like Christ.

CHAPTER 8

Breaking Through Relational Barriers

When Gale Sayers and Brian Piccolo, both running backs for the Chicago Bears, began rooming together in 1967, it was a first for race relations in professional football. It was also a first for both of them. Sayers had never had a close relationship with a white person before—with the possible exception of George Halas—and Piccolo had never really known a black man.

One secret of their growing friendship lay in their similar tastes in humor. Before the 1969 exhibition game in Washington, for instance, an earnest young reporter entered their hotel room for an interview. "How do you two get along?" the writer asked.

"We're OK as long as he doesn't use the bathroom," said Piccolo.

"What do you fellows talk about?" asked the businesslike reporter, ignoring the laughs from the two.

"Mostly race relations," Gale said.

"Nothing but the normal racist stuff," Piccolo added.

"If you had your choice," the writer went on, "who would you want as your roommate?"

Sayers replied, "If you are asking me what white Italian fullback from Wake Forest, I'd have to say Pick."

But submerged beneath the laughter and sarcasm lay a fierce loyalty to each other, and as the movie *Brian's Song* depicted, the friendship between Sayers and Piccolo deepened into one of the best relationships in the history of sports.

Then, during the 1969 season, Piccolo was cut down with cancer. He fought to play the season out, but he was in the hospitals more than he was in the games. Gale Sayers flew to be beside him as often as possible.

They had planned, with their wives, to sit together at the Professional Football Writers annual dinner in New York, where Sayers was to be given the George S. Halas Award as the most courageous player in pro football. But instead, Pick was confined to his bed at home. At the dinner, Sayers stood to receive the award, tears springing to his eyes. The ordinarily terse athlete had this to say as he took the trophy: "You flatter me by giving me this award, but I tell you here and now that I accept it for Brian Piccolo. Brian Piccolo is the man of courage who should receive the George S. Halas Award. I love Brian Piccolo and I'd like you to love him. Tonight when you hit your knees, please ask God to love him, too."[1]

"I love Brian Piccolo." How many times have you heard a man say something like that? Not very often. Yet how much richer would our lives be if we had the courage to declare our affection as Sayers did that night in New York? Of course, to express such affection, we would first have to experience it. And experiencing it would require getting past some major relational barriers men tend to erect. In this chapter I want to identify some of those barriers and develop a strategy to help you get through them.

BARRIER 1: MEISM

In his excellent book *The Hazards of Being a Male*, Dr. Herb Goldberg has a chapter entitled "The Lost Art of Buddyship." In the chapter he notes that in our culture the phenomenon of being without even a single buddy or good friend is a common one—so widespread, in fact, that it's not seen as unusual. Indeed, it seems to be taken for granted.

What's buddyship? It's a relationship in which each man facilitates, and derives deep satisfaction from, the success and achievement of the other. A relationship in which men are open and honest about themselves—their successes, failures, disappointments, and achievements. It's a friendship in which they derive genuine pleasure from just hanging out together.

Why don't we have such relationships as adult men? I believe that the first barrier to buddyship is what I call meism. Of course, as sinners we're all infected with this relational virus. A moment in the movie *Wall Street* illustrates the danger we face. The scene occurs during a large corporate meeting held in a vast room, with hundreds of businesspeople in attendance. Stodgy, anonymous company managers argue with the shareholders for patience, but profits are down. In a sensible world, these forces should be working together with each other. Instead, each special-interest group wants results that will benefit itself.

Finally a corporate leader, played by Michael Douglas, grabs a hand-held microphone and takes over the meeting. Everything about his clothing and his manner tells you he's successful, self-assured, in command. His message boils down to three seductive words: "Greed is good!"

The movie is fictional, but the phrase comes directly from a real-life speech delivered to a group of college students by someone who for a short time was considered one of America's most astute businessmen. He went on to become one of the most famous prisoners of the federal judicial system. Greed caught him when he tried to make millions of dollars illegally as an inside trader.

Greed destroys relationships. It undermines friendships. Why? Because greed prompts us to be self-protective. It drives us to take rather than receive. It causes us to see other men as competitors rather than friends. It prevents us from rejoicing in the success of others, because their accomplishment puts the spotlight on someone else instead of us.

Yet we live in a society in which we're told that greed is good. Jesus hit meism head-on when he said, "Greater love has no one than this, that one lay down his life for his friends" (John 15:13). In God's kingdom, men lay aside their greed and self-protection for the sake of others. Jesus said greed is evil and giving is good. Looking out for yourself is harmful and looking out for others is helpful.

I remember my friend Bill Perkins telling me about the time he had a flash of insight. For years he'd met with a small group of men because *he* needed it. One day, after they hadn't met for a while, he was gripped by a deep concern and love for his friends. In that moment he realized he wanted to meet for them. *They* needed to meet. He realized they needed him to be open and self-revealing. They needed his willingness to share his successes and failures, because it encouraged them to do the same thing. His vulnerability was something they needed.

There are men out there who need you. They need to know about your struggles, disappointments, and successes. But the only way you'll ever experience true buddyship is if you make a commitment to trust Christ to enable you to overcome your self-protective meism. You can take a big step in that direction by daily asking God to help you see how your vulnerability can help others. And when you feel prompted by God to share something that's threatening, go ahead and take a risk. Why? For the sake of your friends. Bury meism. It's one funeral you'll never look back on with regret.

BARRIER 2: FEAR OF BEING CONTROLLED

Few things keep men from developing shoulder-to-shoulder relationships more than a fear of being controlled. A story's told about a boy who found a sparrow with a broken wing in the woods outside his home. He took the bird inside, made a cage for it out of sticks, and patiently nursed it back to health. It wasn't long before he came to love the little creature and began to think of it as his.

Within a month or so the bird's wing healed. Soon it began to try to escape from its cage, flapping its wings and hurling itself against the bars. Seeing this, the boy's father said, "Son, you need to let it go. He'll never be happy in that cage. If you keep him, he'll only get hurt."

Finally the boy agreed with his father and reluctantly took the bird out of the cage and carried it outside. Standing in his front yard, the boy continued to hold the bird.

"Open your hands," the boy's father said. "If you squeeze him tightly enough to prevent his escape, you'll hurt him. You might even kill him."

"But if I open my hand, he'll fly away!" cried the boy.

"Maybe so," answered the father. "On the other hand, if he flies away, someday he may return. But if your fear of losing him causes you to cripple or kill him, you'll lose him for sure. The only way you can ever hold on to something that's free is with an open hand."

The boy slowly opened his hand and the bird flew away. He sadly watched it go and felt a deep loneliness. All day he felt lonely. But the next morning, he was awakened by the sound of chirping and saw a little sparrow sitting on a branch outside his window. The boy didn't know if it was his bird or not, but as he went down to breakfast, he realized his loneliness was gone.

I tell that story because it illustrates the danger of trying to control another person. It also demonstrates how hard—yet fulfilling—it can be to relate to others in a noncontrolling manner. Nothing destroys a friendship faster than a tendency to control. And nothing undermines accountability among men more than the presence of a controlling individual. While it's a characteristic found to some degree in each of us, it's also one we want to harness in ourselves.

To help you do this, I'd like to point out some of the different ways men control others, and then make a few suggestions to help you get past this barrier.

The Bully

This man uses brute emotional, verbal, and physical force to control others. He never hesitates to use intimidation. If he's skilled, he intimidates with nothing more than a look. While he seldom has to actually act out and hurt another person physically, he may occasionally crush someone verbally, just to keep his reputation in place.

Two thousand, five hundred years ago the walls of ancient Jerusalem were a pile of rubble. For 150 years they had been in disrepair. At that time in world history, a city's walls were her last line of defense. Without the wall, the city was vulnerable to attack.

Under the astute leadership of Nehemiah, the people of Jerusalem rallied and began to rebuild the walls. The work hadn't been under way for long when Nehemiah was confronted by an ancient bully named Sanballat. Nehemiah wrote, "When Sanballat heard that we were rebuilding the wall, he became angry and was greatly incensed. He ridiculed the Jews, and in the presence of his associates and the army of Samaria, he said, 'What are those feeble Jews doing? Will they restore their wall? Will they offer sacrifices? Will they finish in a day? Can they bring the stones back to life from those heaps of rubble—burned as they are?'" (Neh. 4:1–2).

That ancient bully intimidated the Jewish people. He tried to control them with fear. Why? Because their strength threatened his ability to control the area. I'm reminded of the story of a man who had just put in a new sidewalk. When he looked out the window and saw the neighborhood kids writing their names in the soft cement, he ran outside and yelled at the kids, telling them, "Get off my sidewalk!"

The man's wife said, "Why did you yell at those kids? I thought you liked them."

The man replied, "I do like kids. In the abstract, not on the concrete."

Sanballat was like that. He didn't mind the Jewish people as long as they were where he wanted them. When they stepped over the line and began doing something he didn't like, he tried to control them through intimidation. Some men do that nowadays, too. They use the threat of withdrawing their money, friendship, or influence to control other men. Others are hot-tempered and keep those around them under control with the threat of exploding in a rage.

Of course, Nehemiah didn't stand for such bullying tactics for a moment. And neither should we. We shouldn't tolerate it in others or in ourselves.

The Worrywart

A number of years ago I worked with a man who left nothing to chance. He walked around with a three-by-five card in his shirt pocket. Every time he thought of something he or others needed to do, he pulled out the card and wrote it down. He managed to drag out personal and staff meetings by constantly reviewing every detail of everything in the world—or so it seemed.

There are few biblical examples that are better than that of Rebekah. Before the birth of her twin sons, God promised Rebekah that the older, Esau, would serve the younger, Jacob (Gen. 25:23). Years later when the two had become men, Rebekah wanted to help God out. She wanted to make sure

Jacob got the blessing from his father, Isaac. Instead of trusting God, she devised a detailed plan that enabled Jacob to trick his father into blessing him instead of Esau.

Jacob allowed himself to be controlled by a worrywart who felt she had to make sure everything was done according to her plans. While I used a woman to illustrate the point, plenty of men use the same tactic to control others. And when they don't get their way, they may pout or emotionally disconnect from those around them—another attempt to control.

The Takeover Artist

Some people assume they have the right or the duty to take over anything someone else is doing. They command and instruct in order to get behind the steering wheel. They push others aside verbally, emotionally, or physically. Ultimately those around them will find themselves in a position they don't really want to be in. Later if someone makes a fuss about their unwanted role, the takeover artist will be offended.

Peter tried this trick with Jesus when they were on their way to Jerusalem. The Lord had just said he had to go to Jerusalem to die. Peter took Jesus aside and said, "Never, Lord! . . . This shall never happen to you!" (Matt. 16:22). The Lord responded with a harsh rebuke for both Peter and Satan, who had put the idea in Peter's mind.

LETTING GO

As I mentioned before, we all try to control others at one time or another. And we use a variety of tactics to control them. If you want other men to stand shoulder to shoulder with you, you need to identify the techniques you use to control them. And you need to be willing to open your hands and release them.

A number of years ago extensive research was done by George and Nena O'Neill in preparation for their book *Open Marriage*. In talking with hundreds of people in all types of relationships, they discovered that people long for two things. First, they want a relationship with someone. Second, they want their freedom. The best friendships make room for both.

I've discovered several techniques that help me let others know I'm not trying to control them. First, I'm cautious with criticism. A parent who constantly criticizes a child is trying to control the child's behavior. The same is true of a friend. Realizing that, I always try to hand out more affirmation than criticism.

Second, I encourage my friends to be themselves. Instead of trying to fit them into a mold I've built for them, I appreciate their uniqueness. The strongest teams are made up of men with different talents. What kind of football team would you have if every player was an Emmitt Smith? He's a great running back, but he wouldn't get very far without some three-hundred-pound linemen to open up those running lanes.

Third, encourage your friends to have other relationships. None of us have exclusive rights to anybody. Just because a buddy has other friends doesn't mean you're not still a close friend, too.

Fourth, allow for changes in the relationship. I know of a man—I'll call him Bob—who for years served as a subordinate at work to his best friend. Over time Bob's career blossomed, and he ended up in a position of greater influence than his friend. Everything had shifted. For a while Bob wondered how his buddy would respond to the change. In fact, he wondered how *he* would respond. Because of the depth of their friendship, they became even closer. Some men can't handle such shifts, because it changes the balance of power. But in a noncontrolling friendship, such shifts aren't threatening.

Of course, these barriers aren't something we climb over and then never have to deal with again. Getting past them is a process. And as you're working to deal with your meism and harness your tendency to control, there are a couple more barriers you need to be aware of.

BARRIER 3: FEAR OF REJECTION

Several years ago I was having a severe struggle that was triggering both anger and depression. When I came home from work, I felt like kicking my dogs and withdrawing from my wife. Instead, I just watched TV. A few of my close friends knew something was wrong, but they weren't sure what. And I was reluctant to tell them, because I feared they would reject me. Even though I knew they wouldn't, that fear prevented me from opening up.

When I'd pretty much reached rock bottom, a close buddy—one that I knew would accept me no matter what—visited me. As we talked, I poured out my guts. He listened and assured me of his love and support. He helped me see that things weren't as bad as I feared, and challenged me to open up with others.

I have to tell you, I'm amazed that with my theological training, my psychological training, and my counseling experience, I still fear rejection. I know God accepts me. I know my close buddies accept me. I know my wife accepts me. I know my dogs accept me. But I still struggle with the fear of rejection.

And you know what else? So do you. Every man fears rejection. That's why as soon as we establish some kind of accountability relationship, we fear that our weaknesses will be exposed and we'll be rejected.

It may surprise you to discover that there's nothing you can do to endear yourself to others more than opening up and being vulnerable. If you'll build more windows and fewer walls, you'll have more shoulder-to-shoulder friends. We all need at least one person to whom we can tell everything.

Not only will your self-disclosure draw others to you, it'll create the kind of environment in which they'll feel free to remove their masks. If you'll dare to take the initiative in self-revelation, other men will be more likely to reveal their secrets to you.

Jesus did this. He prayed with his disciples, walked with them, ate with them, resolved their arguments, and *cried* with them. The one thing most of us would never do around another man, Jesus did. Why? So they could see inside him.

Having said all this about transparency, I'm not suggesting you suddenly tell a person everything the first time you meet. Instead, I'd suggest you gradually pull back the layers, allowing them to respond in kind. Friendships take time to develop. And they develop best with men who are continually getting past their fear of rejection and allowing others to see who they are behind the mask.

BARRIER 4: FEAR OF EXPOSURE

Not only do I want to be accepted, I want to be respected by my friends and my community. It's one thing to open up with a buddy about my struggles, but I don't want them announced on the evening news.

There are two sides to this coin. On one side, I want my secrets to be guarded by my friends. On the other side, I want others to know I can keep their secrets. Few things demonstrate a deepening friendship like the sharing of secrets. As I mentioned above, as you share parts of yourself, your friends will tell you things that you could use to hurt them by telling others. Chances are, your friends will wait to see how you handle what they've given you before they tell you anything more.

If you want to overcome your fear of exposure, share a secret with a friend and see how he responds. If he maintains your confidence and tells you something about himself, take another step.

Every men's group I've ever been a part of has made it a fundamental rule that what's shared with the group goes no further. That means it isn't shared with our wives or other friends. It stays in the group. It's a good idea to never even let others know you're the recipient of someone else's secrets. That's not always so easy, because we want people to know we're a trusted friend. The best way to be a trusted friend is to keep a confidence and not let others know we're doing so.

One summer three pastors went on a mini-retreat at the California coast. It seems a member of one of their churches had a home on the beach and let them use it for the weekend. While they were enjoying dinner, one of the ministers said, "I need to clear my conscience. I've just got to tell you guys something." After that introduction he had their attention. With the other two listening, the pastor continued, "I've been having an affair for three years."

After offering words of support, the second minister said, "I've also got a confession to make. I've stolen one hundred thousand dollars from the church." His friends expressed their comfort and concern.

Things got quiet after dinner, because the third pastor pretty much kept to himself. The next morning as the three were eating breakfast, the two who had confessed their sins told the third, "Hey, we both told you about our secret sin. Now what's yours?"

The third pastor looked at them with absolute seriousness and said, "Mine's gossip, and I can't wait to get home."

That's not the guy you want in your group. And he's not the guy you want to emulate. You want to be the kind of man that will help others overcome their fear of exposure. How? By keeping their secrets.

I'LL HAVE TO CHANGE

Tim Allen has done a great job articulating the passion men have for tools. Time and again, in his television series *Home Improvement,* Tim falls in love with a saw, hammer, drill, gas blower, or some other tool. And he exhibits both determination and skill (although both are amusingly distorted) in fixing things.

As men, we like to fix things. Some of you are better at it than others (notice that I said "you," not "us"). While I don't claim to be any great mechanic, I do like to tinker with my computer and put together things I order through the mail. Especially when they come with instructions I can decipher. Even though I haven't devoted my life to fixing things, as Tim has, I think I could learn how to fix most things, *if* I set my mind to it.

In light of the male propensity to fix things, it's interesting that we can so diligently put off fixing ourselves. We've somehow trained ourselves to postpone this important job. The truth is, problems in the way we think and act don't just go away. They get fixed as a result of years of hard work and strong relationships. They get fixed because men decide to take up their cross and follow Jesus. They decide that following him and becoming like him is the most important thing in life. And if we want to be like Jesus, we have to allow his Spirit to change us.

I mentioned earlier that accountability isn't someone else telling me what I need to do to grow. It's me sharing with them where I want to go and how I want to get there and then giving them permission to check up on me. It's the guardrail on a curvy road that keeps me on track.

The trick is this: For others to indicate a willingness to change, they need me to demonstrate the same willingness. At times we all need to serve as the pace runner—the one who sets the pace in a long race by running fast for a few laps. When we tire or get discouraged, someone else on the team needs to serve in that role.

Shoulder-to-shoulder relationships help us overcome our natural tendency to allow the broken parts of our lives to remain in disrepair. There are men right now who need you to show them how to get past the barriers that cause them to resist change. None of us can get where God wants us without a willingness to change.

I WANT TO BE LIKE THAT

In the book *Chicken Soup for the Soul,* Dan Clark tells a story about a friend of his named Paul, who received a car from his brother as a Christmas present. On Christmas Eve when Paul came out of his office, a boy was walking around the shiny new car, admiring it. "Is this your car, mister?" he asked.

Paul nodded. "My brother gave it to me for Christmas."

The boy was astounded. "You mean, your brother gave it to you, and it didn't cost you nothing? Boy, I wish . . ." The street urchin hesitated.

Of course, Paul knew what he was going to wish for. He was going to wish he had a brother like that. But what the boy said jarred Paul all the way down to his heels.

"I wish," the boy went on, "that I could be a brother like that."[2]

Developing a shoulder-to-shoulder relationship isn't so much a matter of finding the right guys as it is becoming the right guy. It's a matter of becoming a man who, like the boy on the street, wants to give something to his brother, something that will allow him to experience the kind of friendship that will help him become all he wants to be—and all God wants him to be.

Hopefully, someday you'll remember the words of Gale Sayers and know you've got friends just like that, friends who stand shoulder to shoulder with you because together you worked past the barriers that could've limited your friendship.

DISCUSSION QUESTIONS

1. In elementary school, kids were paired up in a "buddy system." What were the reasons for that? Have your basic needs changed that much from elementary school?

2. "Greed destroys relationships." Read the following verses and discuss how this principle worked out: 1 Samuel 18:12, 15, 28–29; 20:30–34. How did this relationship finally end? Compare Saul's actions with Jonathan's.

3. Think about the small group you're in, or the friends you have. What do you have to offer these men? Next, go through the group and identify the unique offering of everyone in the group.

4. Identify which area of control you are most likely to use. (If you're having trouble identifying it, ask your small group—chances are, they've already identified it!)

5. Compare the stories of Nehemiah and Rebekah. What did Rebekah lose by controlling the situation? What did Nehemiah gain?

6. What kinds of things make up your mask (for instance, happiness to mask depression, self-righteousness to mask addiction)? What layer can you begin peeling away? How can you do that? Remember, if you take the initiative, others will follow.

7. Dr. Cooper wrote, "We have trained ourselves to 'postpone' this important job [of fixing ourselves]." Why is this (remember the defense mechanisms in chapter 1)?

8. What kind of brother do you want to be?

Chapter 9

What Works for You

'd just graduated from seminary with my Ph.D. in clinical and counseling psychology. I was delighted to receive an offer from a church where I'd been counseling as part of my graduate program. I was offered the position of pastor of family ministries. Also, as an added bonus, I was going to be working with one of my very best friends—Bill. He was the senior pastor, and our dream had been to serve together in a ministry one day. Our dream came true. We thought that we knew each other pretty well and that me being accountable to him for my responsibilities in the church would not be a big deal. Boy, were we wrong.

Bill's personality style is one of directness and boldness, almost like the Nike commercial—"Just do it!" Bill can be very compassionate, but he can also be very persistent when he wants something. And when he wants something, he wants it now. On the other hand, I'm very analytical and deliberate. I don't like to be pushed into anything, and the harder I'm pushed, the more resistant I'll become. Do not—I repeat, do not—force me to make a decision immediately. If you do, I'll walk out on you.

Bill and I found this out the hard way. I usually went into Bill's office each day to just check in with him and shoot the breeze. One day when I went there, I could tell he wanted to talk about something. Apparently, the small groups weren't starting as fast as the deacons of the church had anticipated. You see, starting the small groups was part of my responsibilities. Bill was feeling pressure to give the deacons an answer, and before I knew it, I was on the hot seat. Bill wanted answers and began to hone in on me with one direct question after another. I needed time to think and began to walk away. Bill said, "Look, Rod, we need to talk this out. Don't leave. Let's talk."

I looked at him with an icy stare and said, "Back off, mister. Leave me alone. I need time to think. I'll get back with you later."

Bill was wise to give me the time I needed. I felt as if I'd been ambushed. Also, I prided myself on my competence, and each of his questions that I couldn't answer made me feel incompetent. Well, I did get back to Bill two days later with answers. We had a good laugh and learned a lot about one another. Bill realized that I do not like surprises. I need time to think so I can give a reasonable answer. I rarely shoot from the hip. Bill's a verbal processor. He needs to talk it out and bring immediate resolution.

We knew that if I was going to be accountable to Bill, he needed to understand how I was wired and how to approach me concerning key issues. Also, I needed to understand Bill's personality style, how best to communicate to him, and how to hold him accountable in our relationship. We needed to understand each other if we were going to be effective in our relationship as partners in the ministry.

The same holds true in shoulder-to-shoulder relationships when it comes to accountability. There's no one-size-fits-all approach when it comes to holding a person accountable. There must be a basic understanding of how the person is wired, the needs he has, and the environment necessary for me to effectively hold him accountable. All of us enter relationships with certain expectations. This is especially true when we talk about being accountable to one another.

Before I go any further, let me define what I mean by accountability. I want to thank Stu Weber for his insights in this area. Accountability is you giving me your permission to ask the hard questions in key areas of your personal and spiritual life. Accountability is me helping you get where you say you want to go. If I see you heading toward the edge, I'm there as a guardrail to keep you from going over. Accountability is not a club with which I beat you into submission. I've found that confrontation without a committed relationship breeds destruction and failure. Accountability is freedom-granting; it keeps the secrets out so a man will not be bound up by them and slip back into isolation.

The Lord himself does not deal with all of us in the same way. He worked differently with Moses than he did with Paul. "Love your neighbor as yourself" (Matt. 22:39) means seeking to understand him so you can truly minister effectively to him and ask the hard questions in such a way that it facilitates his growth rather than hinders it.

Don't get me wrong. I'm not saying we all have to be minicounselors to hold each other accountable. But it doesn't hurt to have a basic understanding of my brother so I can approach him in the best way possible.

Bill didn't deliberately set out to upset me. He was just being himself. But the way he approached me set up a very tense environment rather than a loving one. No two people and their reactions are alike. But even though we are distinctive, we do have predictable behavior patterns. Conflicts develop when the expectations of one person clash with the expectations of another. This does not mean that conflict necessarily has to result when people with different expectations are together. No, if we can improve our awareness and acceptance of the differences between us, we can learn to respond to each other in a positive instead of a negative way. Trust can then be developed, and hard things can be said to one another when necessary, because each one feels understood and safe.

What I'm going to share with you next revolutionized the relationship between Bill and me. Our eyes really opened up when we practiced these principles. Our respect for one another grew, our love deepened, and we were more committed to walk shoulder to shoulder, because we took the time not only to hold one another accountable but to do so in a way that demonstrated that we really understood each other.

A TOOL FOR UNDERSTANDING

There are many personality profiles and categories on the market. As a counselor, I've worked with many of them. Yet the one I've found most helpful was discovered by a counselor in the 1930s by the name of William Martson. Called the DISC model, it's a trait-based description of four behavior styles into which, Martson believed, all persons fall. This system has gone through five generations of refinement, which resulted in a common language to describe behavior. The four key categories are: *D* (dominance), *I* (influence), *S* (steadiness), and *C* (compliance). There are various combinations of these categories, but for our purposes we'll deal with each one in its purest form.

For each personality style, I'm also going to show you

1. Basic motivation
2. What they expect from others
3. Major strengths and weaknesses
4. Best environment for confrontation

5. Behavior under stress
6. What they need others to provide
7. What they need to trust God for
8. Areas for growth

One word of warning. As you learn about personality styles, you'll learn the labels associated with each. By no means do we want to label one another and therefore typecast each other. The personality trait descriptions should not be used to pigeonhole someone or, conversely, to excuse ourselves for not changing our behavior or for resisting accountability. If a label helps clarify differences, it's useful, but if it's used to create barriers to communication, it's confining. This material is meant to help clarify, not confine. Let's take a look at the key categories.

MEMBERS OF THE GROUP

The D Personality

Jim's a D personality. He's a no-nonsense kind of guy. He calls them as he sees them. He's a trial lawyer and very good at what he does. In fact, he can be rather intimidating. Once he sets his mind on something, either get on board or get out of the way.

D stands for dominance. The basic motivation for a D personality is to have results and freedom to act. They are incredibly task oriented and want results. These individuals do not like restrictions, nor do they like to be told what they can't do.

D's have high expectations of others but tend to give themselves slack if they are not measuring up. The strength of the D is that they get things done and are decisive and persistent. The weakness of the D is that they can be insensitive to others and impatient, not listen well, and come across as not needing anyone.

D's want an environment that will challenge them and give them freedom and variety. Under stress they can become autocratic—almost like a dictator. What do they need from others? They need help in being sensitive, friends who will point out cautions if they continue down a certain path, and details and facts. What do *D*'s need to trust God for in their life? Patience and sensitivity to others' needs. Not everybody moves as fast as they do. The task is not as important as the relationship and being more flexible and open. *D*'s can be pretty stubborn.

But what happens when you have to confront a *D*? Let's say Jim comes to our small group and is struggling in his marriage. The last three times you have been together, Jim has mentioned that he feels his wife is shallow and dull. They are just not communicating and he's really frustrated. He has also mentioned how the new administrative assistant he has hired is not only pretty but smart. Jim says that she understands him and that their times at lunch have been great. As a group, you see red flags everywhere, but Jim insists there's nothing happening. How do you hold Jim accountable? How do you approach him and tell him he's heading down a path of destruction?

The best way to lovingly confront Jim is to

1. Be firm and direct
2. Focus on actions and goals
3. Be brief and to the point
4. Do it as a group, not individually, or he'll think it's just your problem
5. Help him formulate a strategy
6. Give him time to think

This really happened. I was in a group in Houston, and Jim (not his real name) needed confronting. When the group started, we let Jim know that he was being insensitive to his wife and not really working on his marriage as he'd promised. He at first became very defensive, but we pointed out how he'd mentioned his administrative assistant three times and how he always seemed to brighten up when he talked about her. Jim exploded and said we were nuts and needed to stay out of his business. He was a big boy and didn't need our help. We were direct and said he needed to put a stop to it. Jim couldn't outtalk all three of us. We asked Jim to think about what we had said, and told him we would discuss it at our next group meeting. Jim came back the next week and reluctantly agreed that we were right. He asked if we would help him.

We helped him formulate a strategy, first of all by telling him to get marriage counseling. Also, we prohibited any more lunches with his administrative assistant and promised we would call him daily to find out how he was doing. Jim balked, but when his marriage improved and he got back on track, he thanked us.

There's a person in Scripture who was a lot like Jim. His name was Paul. In fact, in Acts 9 you'll see that the strategy we used with Jim was the very same one Jesus used with Paul. Jesus used a strong confrontational approach, presented him with the facts, gave him time to think, and then restored him. Yet once Paul got the message, the enthusiasm he once had against the gospel was channeled into proclamation of the gospel. Once Paul saw his need to change, he "just did it," and change came quickly.

The I Personality

Bob's an adventurer. He loves to laugh, relate, and take risks. He also has the attention span of a gnat. He constantly moves from one project to another and rarely completes any of them. He usually doesn't do his homework and almost always has a funny story to share. He's a warm and charming guy who has never met a stranger. By the way, Bob's one of the top-producing salesmen in his company. Bob's an *I* personality.

You'll find that the *D* and the *I* personalities have a very hard time adapting to their environment. If they can change it, they will. The *D* will do so by force of character, while the *I* will do it by being incredibly relational.

I stands for influence. The basic motivation of the *I* personality is recognition and social approval. It's incredibly important for an *I* to be liked—even if it means telling you a lie to stay in your good graces. Can you see where accountability would be difficult for this person?

I's have low expectations of themselves and of others. In other words, if you fudge a little bit, that's not too bad. They have a very wide margin of forgiveness and grace. The strength of *I*'s is that they are optimistic, personable, and enthusiastic. They are truly life's cheerleaders. Their weakness lies in being manipulative, being oversellers of what they can do, and lacking follow-through. And they are not very good listeners. The *I* personality wants an environment that's friendly, warm, free from control and detail, and gives him the opportunity to influence others.

Under stress the *I* can attack. He almost comes across like a *D* but tends to shift the blame much more. You'll hear, "Well, if he'd just done what he was supposed to, I wouldn't have had to lie." The group needs to balance this brother out by helping him follow through, have a logical rather than purely emotional approach to problems, and concentrate on the task.

An *I* personality in Scripture is the apostle Peter. Peter said he would never deny Christ, in Matthew 26:35. Jesus said he would. Later Peter's sitting around the fire, and a servant girl says, "Hey, aren't you one of *his* men?" Peter says no. Another person and then another begin to make this observation, and finally Peter swears that he doesn't know the man Jesus. Remember, *I* personalities hate rejection and can succumb to peer pressure. Not only does Peter's denial fulfill Scripture but it reveals his personality weakness.

What do *I*'s need to trust God for? They need to trust God for objectivity in decision making, patience to pause before acting (and to engage mind before mouth), and better control of time. These folks are event oriented rather than time oriented. Whenever they get there is when things start, and it's over when they leave. This drives the *D* personality nuts.

So how do we, as a group, hold Bob accountable and lovingly confront him when necessary? Let's say that Bob has some important clients in from out of town. They make it clear to Bob that they expect to have a night out on the town, going barhopping and doing whatever suits their fancy. Bob knows this runs totally against the grain of his beliefs but consents to arrange everything and go with them. His plan is to set everything up and then all of a sudden become ill and let them go out on their own. By doing so, he won't have to go and he can still land the big account. So what if he tells a little lie? Nobody gets hurt—right? Bob thinks his idea is a stroke of genius and shares it with you. What do you do? How do you lovingly confront him about his compromising?

The best way I've found to lovingly confront an *I* personality is to

1. Create an environment that's friendly and positive, letting him know you are on his side
2. Use friendly voice tones—no yelling
3. Allow him to verbalize his feelings and fears
4. Express to him that you can understand why he's afraid
5. Transform talk into an organized action plan
6. Offer encouragement and incentives for doing the right thing
7. Communicate affirmation and a belief that he can do it with your help

The way to approach Bob would be to put your hand on his shoulder and say how you empathize with him in this predicament. Then ask him what he's afraid of most. Once he has verbalized his fears, you can remind him of his commitment to honesty and let him know that the group's there to fully support him. Encourage Bob to follow an action plan, which would include telling his clients he doesn't do the sort of things they have in mind and giving them some alternatives. Remind him that in the end he will have pleased God and maintained his integrity. Also, give him a timeline and follow up with him. Bob will be grateful. I know, because I saw a friend of mine like Bob stand up to some very difficult business practices in his company with his shoulder-to-shoulder brothers backing him up.

The S Personality

Mark's a peaceful, sensitive, generous, and sociable kind of guy. He's very amiable and rarely gives his opinion about anything, even when pushed to share. If people need someone who will listen, Mark's their guy. He's also very logical and has the ability to see the big picture. Mark's very visually oriented and loves to watch movies and TV. Mark's also a team player. He works for an architectural firm as one of their draftsmen. Mark's an *S* personality style.

S stands for steadiness. You can always count on the fact that rain or shine, this person is going to be there. The basic motivation for an *S* personality is relationship and appreciation. And the most important relationships for an *S* personality are the ones in his family. Everything else can be falling apart as long as things are fine on the home front. The *S* personality has high expectations for himself but does not really place high demands on those around him. He'll beat himself up quite a bit but will usually let those around him off the hook.

The major strength of this personality style is his ability to support and comfort those around him. He's also very loyal and agreeable. He may not have a lot of friends, but the ones he has are lifelong.

If you were to ask him what his favorite food is, he'd say, "Whatever *you* like." His weakness is that he will conform to those around him, isolate himself, and miss opportunities because of a lack of initiative. The best environment for the *S* personality is one in which he can be part of a team. The environment also has to be one that's consistent—the *S* does not like surprises. Under stress the *S* personality will acquiesce, withdraw into his shell, and become passive-aggressive.

This personality needs others to provide challenge for him. He needs someone to help him stretch out of his comfort zone. He also needs help in solving difficult problems, so he will not feel overwhelmed. He needs someone who will believe in him. In other words, this person lacks a lot of confidence and needs the team to challenge him and instill confidence in him so he can have what it takes to get the job done.

This type of person needs to trust God for facing confrontation. The *S* personality hates confrontation and will sometimes let things build to a crisis point and blow up, rather than deal with the issue. Finally, he needs to be more assertive about stating and pursuing his goals and aspirations. If not, he'll stay stagnant and not grow in his walk with God.

So how does one lovingly confront an *S*?

Mark came to the shoulder-to-shoulder group as usual. In fact, he rarely missed. But something was different. He was visibly shaken. Normally Mark was rather quiet and had a kind of poker face, even when it came to discussing some very difficult subjects. But not tonight. Finally one of the group members assured Mark they wanted to hear from him. Would he share what was going on in his life? Mark's lower lip began to quiver, and in very slow and halting speech he said, "I think Mary's going to leave me."

Mary, Mark's wife, is as outgoing and aggressive as Mark is quiet and agreeable. Mark shared that Mary had been complaining about how they needed more money to make ends meet, especially since Mark had brought his nephew and father to live with their family. Mark told the group that Mary had begged him to ask for a raise at work. He told the group how Mary had pointed out that although he was one of his company's top draftsmen, he hadn't received a pay increase in two years. Why couldn't he go in and ask the boss for a raise?

Mark also told of an incident in which they attended a dinner party and the host misunderstood and began introducing Mary as Mark's sister. Mark never corrected the host, and one of the guests tried to pick her up. Mary got mad and made a scene and walked out. Mark said Mary was still really upset about the incident. He said Mary also resented the fact that when he came home from work each day, he usually retired to the den and watched television until it was time to go to bed. "Mary's had enough and says she's thinking about moving out," Mark said. "My world is my family. If Mary leaves, I don't know what I'll do."

I've found that the best way to lovingly confront and motivate an S personality is to

1. Provide a sincere, personal, nonthreatening environment
2. Show a sincere interest and listen before giving advice
3. Ask "how" questions to get an opinion: "How do you want this to change?"
4. Be patient with him—change may be slow but it'll be sure
5. Present ideas for change in a nonthreatening manner, but give him the facts

    6. Define his role in the plan, making it specific and concrete
    7. Provide personal assurance and support
    8. Emphasize how his actions will minimize his risk

Mark was commended by the group for his openness and courage. He was thanked for not keeping this to himself. The group then asked, "What can we do to help you?" This gave Mark the assurance that he had a team who would support him in taking some difficult steps, especially those that might require confrontation. They pulled in a chalkboard, knowing Mark was visual, and listed the issues, then brainstormed options for each one. For instance, it was agreed that Mark needed to write a letter to Mary, expressing his apologies for not listening to her and for not standing up for her at the party. Also, in the letter he would share his heart for her and promise to be more aggressive in pursuing her needs. The group would help Mark formulate a plan and a timetable for meeting his goals, and hold him accountable.

Mark responded positively, because he knew that these men were his friends. The greatest hurdle for an *S* personality is to set boundaries and deal with conflict. With good men in his life, he can do both.

The biblical counterpart to an *S* personality would be the patriarch Abraham. Remember, Abraham had trouble telling the truth (he introduced his wife to Pharaoh as his sister) and pretty much let Sarah call the shots—hence Ishmael. Yet God was patient, and Abraham ended up being not only commended for his faith but called "God's friend" (James 2:23).

The C Personality

C stands for compliance. "Compliance" in this model means to comply to a very high standard of excellence. In other words, if the scale is one to ten, ten is not only the ideal, it's the goal.

Mr. C. is a seminary professor. His specialized field is marriage and family counseling. Mr. C.'s a perfectionist. He spends hours preparing his lecture, even rehearsing key points in his presentations for class. He's very creative and sees teaching as not merely the dispensing of information but a form of discipleship for his students, a means to help them reach a higher level both personally and professionally. He's loyal, works well with others, and gets the most from his staff and his students. He's very diplomatic and can adjust to whatever situation he may be facing. He's also his own worst critic and puts himself down readily when he makes a mistake. Mr. C. is, of course, a C personality.

The basic motivation for C's is quality assurance and being right. Their motto is, "Let's be reasonable—we'll do it my way." Either the job's done right or it's not worth doing. All or nothing. C's have very high expectations of themselves and others. If they can do it, so can you—no exceptions. There's not a lot of room, if any, for noncompliance in regard to the standard of excellence they set.

The strength of C's is that they are orderly, thorough, and analytical. Their corresponding weakness can be a nitpicky attitude, too much attention to detail, and too much caution when it might be time to move ahead. C's hesitate when making decisions, because they don't want to make a mistake. It's incredibly important for them to be seen as competent. C's want an environment that will be supportive and predictable, is clearly defined, and requires precision.

Under pressure C's will do everything to escape. In fact, they can become incredibly depressed and take on a victim mentality. They'll say, "There's no use trying." What do they need from their shoulder-to-shoulder partners? They need those who will help them stop procrastinating in decision making, give them reassurance, and stretch them to become more spontaneous and flexible.

C's need also to trust God for being more open and laughing at their mistakes. They need to trust God for more self-confidence and optimism. They need to concentrate on doing right things and not so much on doing things right.

How do you hold a *C* accountable and lovingly confront him when necessary? Well, let me tell you what works on me. You see, I'm the Mr. C. mentioned above. The way to lovingly confront a *C* personality is to

1. Be specific and accurate—a *C* needs clear examples
2. Make allowance for initial reactions to be defensive and/or negative
3. Allow freedom to ask questions
4. Answer questions in a patient and persistent manner
5. Mix accurate information with assurance
6. Allow time for him to process the information
7. Provide a step-by-step approach to the goal
8. Provide reassurance of support
9. Do not let him play the victim

In the story of the conflict between Bill and me, you'll recall my anger. I was upset because my competence was being brought into question. As a *C,* I too often live by a list of dos and don'ts. I'm only as good as my last performance. In other words, my value is directly proportionate to my ability to perform. Not good.

As Bill learned about my issues as a *C,* it revolutionized our relationship personally and professionally. Bill assured me that he believed in my ability to start the small groups but said that I needed to set a timetable for the actual implementation of training the group leaders. The questions he asked me weren't accusatory but fact oriented. He pointed out that the deacons weren't questioning my ability either but were anxious to start something the church had needed for a long time. They were glad they had a highly skilled person to pull it off.

I needed to hear that, because as a *C*, I tend to take things too personally rather than keep them in front of me objectively. I came up with a timeline and outlined the resources I would need. Bill then held me to it. When things weren't coming together, I would want to play the victim and say, "Maybe I can't do this." Bill wouldn't hear of it. He'd say, "You can. I'm here. Now keep at it." Through Bill's support and encouragement, the small groups took off without too many problems. Also, Bill gave me a lot of grace and affirmed me apart from my performance. I'm finally beginning to enjoy the grace of God, because I have a friend who models it for me.

A Scripture character who fits this profile is Moses. In Exodus you see God calling Moses to go get his people. In chapter 3 God tells Moses how he has heard the cry of his people and will be with Moses and give Moses what he needs to deliver his people. In chapter 4 Moses lists a series of objections: "What if they don't believe me? Lord, I'm not a good speaker. Maybe you'd better send someone else. I'm not qualified."

In each instance, God provides Moses the needed assurances, like miracles to prove his authenticity and Aaron to help him speak. Finally, God will not let Moses play the victim but simply says, "You da man!" (That's what the original Hebrew said. Just kidding.) Moses then reluctantly goes to do God's bidding. As time goes on, Moses and God become very close.

As you can see, God keeps in mind who we are and sets up an environment that will help us grow and keep us accountable to him. Yet he tailors each situation for each person, keeping in mind the bent, or personality style, he has placed in each one. If we are going to have deep shoulder-to-shoulder relationships, we can afford to do no less.

Lee Iacocca once asked legendary football coach Vince Lombardi what it took to make a winning team. The book *Iacocca* records Lombardi's answer:

> There are a lot of coaches with good ball clubs who know the fundamentals and have plenty of discipline but still don't win the game. Then you come to the third ingredient: if you're going to play together as a team, you've got to care for one another. You've got to love each other. Each player has to be thinking about the next guy and saying to himself, "If I don't block that man, Paul is going to get his legs broken. I have to do my job well in order that he can do his." The difference between mediocrity and greatness is the feeling these guys have for each other.[1]

As we take seriously Jesus' command to love one another, we'll watch out for one another and build a winning team.

DISCUSSION QUESTIONS

1. Read Psalm 139:13–16. Who is responsible for differing personality types? How does that help when it comes to accountability?

2. In your group, discuss accountability. Define it in your own terms. How can your group approach a point at which you are able to hold each other accountable?

3. Discuss the statement "accountability is freedom granting." Do you agree or disagree?

4. Identify what type of personality you may be (remember, no one is a pure type—you may be a combination of traits). Give reasons or examples of your type.

5. As you read through the Bible look at the personality types of the following people: Jacob, Joshua, Deborah, Daniel, Sarah, King Ahab, John the Baptist, the apostle John. Note their failures, their confrontations and how God used them.

6. Dr. Cooper wrote, "... God keeps in mind who we are and sets up an environment that will help us grow and keep us accountable to him." How can you see God's hand throughout your life, orchestrating your growth in him? Discuss how your group can maximize understanding each other in order to help each other grow.

Chapter 10

Accountability and the Stages of Man's Life

One of my favorite movies of all time is *City Slickers*. In the movie, Billy Crystal plays Mitch, who happens to be going through a midlife crisis. When we first see Mitch, he's with his two best friends, Phil and Ed. All three of them are fleeing down the streets of Pamplona, Spain, participating in the famous running of the bulls. Ed and Phil get away but Mitch isn't so lucky. He gets hammered by one of the bulls, right in the butt. This is so painful that for weeks he can't sit down.

This isn't the first time these three have done wild and crazy things to prove their masculinity. For several years they've tried to find ever more exotic ways to prove their masculinity. On the plane ride home from Spain, Phil thinks it would be a great idea if they went skydiving on the next trip.

As we get to know Mitch better, we see that he's a very normal guy. He's married and has a couple of kids and a good job at a radio station, selling airtime to advertisers. Yet Mitch feels depressed and discouraged. He has truly lost his joy and passion for life.

One day he's asked to go to career day at his son's school. The dad who speaks just before Mitch tells harrowing stories about being a construction worker. He tells tales of the danger, daring, and bravery involved in his work. Mitch knows he's up next. How do you make selling air for a radio station brave, exciting, and daring? When he does get up before the kids, here's what I remember him saying:

> Value this time in your life, kids, when you still have your choices. It goes by fast. When you're a teenager, you think you can do anything, and you do. Your twenties are a blur. Thirties, you raise your family, you make a little money, and you think to yourself, "What happened to my twenties?" Forties, you grow a little potbelly, you grow another chin. The music starts to get too loud, one of your old girlfriends from high school becomes a grandmother. Fifties, you have a minor surgery—you call it a procedure but it's a surgery. Sixties, you'll have major surgery, the music is still too loud but it doesn't matter, because you can't hear it anyway.
>
> Seventies, you and the wife retire to Ft. Lauderdale. You start eating dinner at two in the afternoon, you have lunch around ten, breakfast the night before, spend most of your time wandering around malls looking for the ultimate soft yogurt, muttering, "How come the kids don't call?" The eighties, you'll have a major stroke, and you end up babbling with some Jamaican nurse who your wife can't stand but who you call Mama.
>
> Any questions?

Right after this scene, Mitch and his wife figure out that he's truly going through a midlife crisis.

I love this scene, because it depicts—in a rather humorous way—that we do go through stages in life. How we handle the transitions from one stage to another has a lot to do with whether we'll be successful in the next stage or not. To make it safely and successfully from one stage to another, we need our shoulder-to-shoulder brothers to help encourage us and hold us accountable, especially in certain areas. The Bible says, "The glory of young men is their strength, gray hair the splendor of the old" (Prov. 20:29). We find that at different stages, we have certain strengths in our lives, as well as corresponding weaknesses. A twenty-year-old may not need to be accountable for the same things a sixty-year-old needs to be accountable for.

In this chapter I'm going to lay out for you the various stages of a man's life and suggest what things would be important to hold a man accountable for during each stage of life.

There's a critical study on men that has truly influenced my thinking concerning the stages of a man's life. It was Daniel Levinson's book *The Seasons of a Man's Life*. Levinson looks in depth at the lives of forty men and from this research draws a theoretical developmental frame for understanding manhood. His conclusions were very simple: Manhood is reflected differently throughout the life cycle. There exist certain predictable stages and transition points in a man's life. Levinson's structure has really appealed to me because it has fit my own personal experience and the experience of so many men I've counseled.

One of the key contributions of Levinson's work was applying to men the reality that adult life is not static. There are constant changes taking place in our lives, changes that require adjustments along the way. What characterizes and defines a man in his twenties is not the same as what characterizes and defines a man in his forties. Yet both are stages of manhood, and knowing what's appropriate for each stage is important.

I've taken Levinson's work and combined it with that of another stage theorist, a woman by the name of Gail Sheehy, the author of the book *New Passages*. In this way, I feel we can get a pretty clear picture of the stages a man goes through in life, and what he needs from his friends during those times.

We'll be looking at five key stages:

1. The Testing Twenties
2. The Turbulent Thirties
3. The Fickle Forties
4. The Flaming Fifties
5. The Serene Sixties

I'm sure we could come up with other stages and categories, but these general time frames will give us a good idea of the issues involved at each stage.

THE TESTING TWENTIES

This particular period in a man's life is incredibly crucial, because he's laying the foundation for the rest of his life. During this time period the young man is usually either finishing college or in the workforce full-time already. It's during this time that the boy becomes a man. This is also a time of grieving, because he now realizes that he no longer can be considered a child or return home and relate to his parents in the same capacity.

The critical issues a young man faces during this time are:

1. Forming his dreams and determining which career path to follow to fulfill those dreams
2. Forming his occupation
3. Forming love relationships

This is a time of experimentation and exploration to determine which track a man will finally end up running on to achieve his dreams. He may try several occupations during this time period to see what he's really good at in life.

He desires to keep all his options open and avoid making strong relational commitments and may flit from one girlfriend to another. This is a time for him to flex his muscles, so to speak. This is also a real roller-coaster time in a man's life, because he wants to create a stable foundation for his life and yet wants very much to explore as well. This is also a time when his values will be put to the test.

A man at this stage of life needs shoulder-to-shoulder brothers who will be mentors to him and give him a sense of security, stability, and confidence. A Testing Twenties man will be prone to depression and discouragement, because he's trying to find his niche in life and find his mate. He may seek to find relief through various means, such as sex, and will face a lot of peer pressure to compromise his values. He needs brothers who will show confidence in him and encourage him to hang in there. He also needs men who will hold him accountable and remind him of his commitment to purity and integrity in relationships with the opposite sex. If the young man gets married during this time, he's going to need role models who will help him when he hits those difficult times in his marriage.

Jim's twenty-three years old, has been out of college for three years, and just got married. We get together regularly. I remember asking him what he felt he needed from our shoulder-to-shoulder times. He said, "Rod, just help me sort through the confusion. When I'm beginning to wonder about my ability to make it, please be there to walk with me. I not only need a friend, I need an older brother who will give me guidance and get in my face when I start to get too cocky, like I've arrived. Help me harness my energy for Christ's sake." I love Jim and see him struggling, but I also see him growing as a man of integrity.

THE TURBULENT THIRTIES

Research seems to indicate that when a man reaches his thirties, a greater sense of urgency is present. Life's becoming more restrictive, more serious, more for real. A man in this stage has the feeling that if there are things he doesn't like or things missing that he would like to have, this is the time to make changes or it'll soon be too late. He's also in the throes of having a family and taking on the responsibilities of being a father as well as establishing his career and settling down.

It's during this stage that a man zeroes in on his niche in society and becomes productive and competent in his chosen endeavors. Here's where he really gets serious about fulfilling his dreams. He works to "make it" and tries to build a better life for himself and his family.

It's also during this stage that a man is more vulnerable, because to get up the ladder, he must rely on others. He feels very much out of control and dependent but wants very much to be in control and independent. There's also the reality that the old gray stallion ain't what he used to be. At this time a man starts getting in touch more than ever with his own mortality and physical limitations.

Levinson puts it well when he says,

At the start of this period, a man is on the bottom rung of his ladder and is entering a world in which he is a junior member. His aims are to advance in the enterprise, to climb the ladder and become a senior member in that world. His sense of well-being during this period depends strongly on his own and others' evaluation of his progress.

At the end of this stage, from about age thirty-six to forty, there is a distinctive phase that we call Becoming One's Own Man. The major developmental tasks of this phase are to become a senior member in one's world, to speak more strongly with one's voice, and to have a greater measure of authority.

This is a fateful time in a man's life. Attaining senior-ity and approaching the top rung of his ladder are signs to him that he is becoming a man (not just a person, but a male adult). Although his progress brings new rewards, it also carries the burden of greater responsi-bilities and pressures. It means that he must give up even more of the little boy within himself.[1]

The key issue with which a man in this stage of life will need help from his shoulder-to-shoulder brothers is summed up in one word: "balance." A man in his Turbulent Thirties can become so concerned with making it careerwise that he'll justify disconnecting from his family and friends to pursue financial independence. Now don't misunderstand me—there's nothing wrong with wanting to provide the best possible living for your family. But provision is more than providing financially. Provision also means providing your presence physically and emotionally.

It's during this stage that a man must make sure that he's investing his life not only in his work but in his family and friends as well. Shoulder-to-shoulder friends help a man in this stage stay connected with his family and friends, as well as cheer him on in his career. Our shoulder-to-shoulder brothers can help us keep our perspective, by asking us the hard ques-tions, like, "When is enough enough?" and "What are you going to take with you into eternity?"

I remember working with a pastor who was doing great work in his community. He was really succeeding in his denominational circle and was beginning to build a reputation nationally. He came to see me because his wife was threatening to leave and his children were unhappy. He discovered he was so busy that he had no shoulder-to-shoulder friends. He said, "Rod, I've finally realized that I've put my family on the shelf more than my books." He was able to reconnect with his family and now has some good brothers who are helping him monitor his schedule so he won't get into this predicament again. In fact, he has to bring his schedule to his small group so they can call him to account concerning other key areas in his life. A man during this stage needs to strive for balance and have brothers around who will hold him accountable.

THE FICKLE FORTIES

On February 5, 1947, Adlai Stevenson wrote in his diary, "Am forty-seven today . . . What's the matter? Have everything. Wife, children, money, success."

The forties are fickle because a man has reached the peak of productivity and achievement potential and yet feels more insecure and depressed than ever before in his life. This is the stage at which a man stops and reevaluates his values and purpose in life. He has climbed a mountain peak and now looks in both directions and asks, "Do I feel fulfilled?" We've often called this stage the midlife crisis. I believe that this difficult time can be a transition rather than a crisis if a man has shoulder-to-shoulder brothers to help him through.

I thought that by being a counselor and helping other men through this period of their lives, I would be spared. Not! I remember waking up one night in a cold sweat, realizing I was forty-one years old and had lived possibly more than half my life. Let me tell you what I felt. I felt depressed, indecisive, confused, and obsessed about what I was going to do with the rest of my life. I experienced self-pity and the feeling of being trapped. I had a hard time sleeping and eating and found myself being very angry and rebellious because I might not get to fulfill my dreams. In fact, I found myself angry at God, because I'd always been the "good boy." I felt God owed me for my faithfulness, and it didn't seem to be panning out as I'd envisioned. If it hadn't been for my shoulder-to-shoulder friends, I might have done some things I would have regretted.

I believe a man is incredibly vulnerable during this stage. In fact, let me share with you six key reasons this stage is so difficult for a man.

1. *Biological changes.* A man begins to lose vigor, muscle tone, and hair. There's a weight shift and less testosterone. In other words, a man usually becomes less sexually stimulated. I've found, as a counselor, that when a woman reaches her forties, she wants to have sex because it proves she's still desirable to her husband. But her husband has less desire for sex, because of his depression and because he's using all his energies to break out of his confusion.

2. *Psychological changes.* A man's ego and self-image are affected, because he wonders what he can still do to somehow salvage his dreams.

3. *Social changes.* A man knows he cannot afford to make any key changes in his life careerwise because of his age. He also begins to reevaluate his relationship to his wife, children, career, and friends.

4. *Family pressures.* A man's children are at the ages in which their lives and activities are highly demanding, and his parents' needs are increasing.

5. *Financial pressures.* Teenagers are costly (clothes, gas, insurance), college is expensive, and parents may need help financially.

6. *Work pressures.* A man may face the fear of being laid off or being overlooked for a promotion. He also finds

himself having low energy reserves and no time for art, music, or contemplation, and he feels he can't change jobs, for reasons of financial security.

These reasons cause a man to feel trapped, and we can do desperate things when we feel trapped. I've seen men frantically trying to Rogaine—excuse me—regain their youth by growing their hair back and trying to get in shape. Others will exchange the necktie and suit with open-collared, bright polos and gold necklaces. Still others might start focusing on leisure activities, from buying a sports car to taking exotic fishing and hunting trips.

But tragically, others may have an affair. Many men have mistakenly tried this route to solve the trauma of lost youth and masculinity. Let me be frank—it's not worth it. Don't take my word for it. Just ask a man by the name of David, king of Israel. The Bible says that "at the time when kings go off to war, David . . . remained in Jerusalem" (2 Sam. 11:1). David was at his midlife and too valuable to be taking risks as he did as a younger man.

David was a man well acquainted with living his life by physical power. As a young man, he'd defeated a giant by the name of Goliath and had fended off wild bears and lions to protect his flocks. Through his late teens and twenties, he was in exile and forced to live in the wilderness, depending on his physical strength and wit for survival. Now he was the king, the administrator of the kingdom. He was restless and couldn't sleep. He decided to take a walk, and as he peered down on the roofs from his balcony at the palace, he saw a woman bathing. You know what happened next. David was ripe for an affair. A one-night stand turned out to have some pretty dire consequences. It ended with the woman, Bathsheba, pregnant, her husband, Uriah, murdered, David's general, Joab, compromised, and a wonderful, godly man, David, never ever fully the same.

What are the consequences of having an affair?

1. It creates dual personalities—you have one with the mistress and one with the wife.
2. It creates stress caused by trying to keep from getting caught.
3. It creates emotional involvements and attachments.
4. It creates humiliation when you get caught.
5. It creates guilt—David ended up having to confess (Ps. 32:3–5).

All this happened to David. Read 2 Samuel 11:1–27 and you'll see that it's not worth it. In fact, David's shoulder-to-shoulder brother Nathan held David accountable and then walked him through his pain and helped him experience the forgiveness of God (2 Sam. 12:1–14).

What must a man do to get through this stage whole and holy? How can his shoulder-to-shoulder brothers help him? I believe there are six keys to weathering this stage successfully.

1. *Focus on what's left—not what's lost.* Realize that you have only played the first half of your life and that with the proper adjustments, you can win the game in the second half. Henry Ford was practically broke and unknown at forty. He later raised twenty-eight thousand dollars to establish the Ford Motor Company. The rest is history. Robert Frost published his first book of poetry at age forty. Winston Churchill was considered a washed-up politician at forty. He became the prime minister of England at sixty-five. Recognize that your greatest contributions are yet to be made.

2. *Concentrate on God.* Carl Jung, a counselor, once said that the root of mental illness among his patients over the age of thirty-five was a loss of spiritual moorings.

Get to know God—not just about him. Begin to look at your view of God and see if it's healthy. Pray and read the Word and ask God to come to you in a fresh way. Experience his grace and know that there's "no condemnation for those who are in Christ Jesus" (Rom. 8:1). This is when our shoulder-to-shoulder brothers can help us, by loving us through this time of barrenness.

3. *Focus on relationships.* Take the time to play with your wife and children. Begin to invest in memories through vacations and special trips. Spend more time with your shoulder-to-shoulder friends by sharing your pain and your joy. Take trips with your brothers and enjoy them.

4. *Find a hobby and get into shape through exercise and diet.* A study by Professor Ismail of Purdue found that middle-aged men who exercised and had outside interests became more emotionally stable and self-confident. Never stop growing and expanding your horizons.

5. *Keep an eternal perspective.* Begin doing those things that contribute to people. God has called us to love people and use things. Remember, relationships are the only things with eternal value. Begin doing those things that will leave a legacy.

6. *Know that this is a stage.* It may seem like forever in getting through this time. But do not force it to happen—let it happen. Corrie ten Boom said, "When you are in a train and going through a tunnel you do not jump out. No, you stay in the train car as it is going through the tunnel and trust the conductor to get you through to the other side." Trust the Conductor—he knows where he is going, even when you don't.

This is the stage at which a man really needs his brothers. As brothers, hold your friend accountable by encouraging him, reminding him, and warning him of those issues mentioned above.

I thank God for my shoulder-to-shoulder brothers. There have been times I've just wanted to go out and blow it. Buy a new car, look at pornography, or just give up. But my brothers have been there to remind me that God has great plans for me—that it's only halftime, and as a team, we'll play the second half together. Praise God for my brothers.

THE FLAMING FIFTIES

The marks of a man who has successfully made it through the Fickle Forties are seen in his Flaming Fifties. Those characteristics are:

1. *An increase in productivity.* It's as if he has gotten his second wind and is ready to run a few more laps.
2. *A decrease in competitiveness.* There's a greater desire to connect and make solid relationships, especially among his family and friends.
3. *A greater desire to help people.* He no longer sees things in a strictly utilitarian way—"What's in it for me?" He now asks, "What can I do for you?"
4. *An ability to enjoy leisure.* He looks for opportunities to enjoy life and not just survive it. He's no longer restless on his days off—he's learned to rest.
5. *An ability to be alone.* His life's not cluttered up with busyness, which made him barren. He now takes the time to get alone and think, pray, and meditate. I have a good buddy who every year takes his annual "journey." He has a special place in California where he'll go for a week—alone. He goes there to pray and

think. He says this time reminds him of what truly is important in life. I've seen his life—it works.

6. *Marriage is more satisfying.* A man in this stage realizes that his wife truly is a gift from God. He focuses in on her, knowing that they are going to finish the race together.

Gail Sheehy, in her book *New Passages,* seems to confirm these observations. She says,

> The 110 Professional Men I've studied have reached an average age of fifty-two. Most at this age feel closer than ever before to their wives. They are also hungry for closer contacts with their children and a different level of friendship with other men and women. The edge of competitiveness has softened.

> If these men were ranked on mental health, most of them would get an A at this stage. Nearly all have developed passions or hobbies that happily occupy and challenge them outside their workaday routines.... This was not true in their mid-forties, when almost half went through a depressive period. Now they are more open to discovering the emotional parts of themselves that didn't fit with the posture of the tough, combative, straight-ahead, rational men they were supposed to be.... The healthy ones recognize the presence of an inner life and start paying attention to its muffled messages.

> As their power orientation subsides in their fifties, the happiest men grow noticeably more expressive and sensuous, more gregarious and likable. Once they are able to satisfy the heightened need for human closeness they formerly suppressed, they are able to be

more perceptive in their reactions to other people. This makes them more valuable as managers, husbands, fathers and friends. They are now able to move toward intimacy with others and a sense of personal meaning in life.[2]

This is great, but how did these men get there? Sheehy points out that they "reached out to men's groups and spiritual guides"[3] to help them keep their focus. A man who successfully enters this stage of life doesn't need accountability as much as he needs to be there for others in the group. His newfound freedom in life and in the Lord serves as an example of what a man has to look forward to in his life. He can get through the Fickle Forties whole and holy.

I have a friend—let's call him Brady—who is having the time of his life. He's fifty-five years old. This man grabs life by the throat and lives it to its fullest. He laughs hard, plays hard, and works hard. He truly loves his wife and child and visibly demonstrates it through tears of joy. He has also been my biggest cheerleader as I go through the Fickle Forties. He's a rock. Every week, we meet in a shoulder-to-shoulder group, and he never fails to help me stay focused and faithful. He also does not judge me. He has compassion first, *then* he gives his sage wisdom. Men in their Flaming Fifties need accountability for normal issues, like daily time with God, Bible study, time with family, and so on. Yet these men can truly be a beacon light to those men who are in the midst of their dark tunnels of life. Thank God for the Bradys in life.

THE SERENE SIXTIES

A man knows he has reached late adulthood when (1) he reaches down to straighten his sock and finds he isn't wearing any, and (2) his children look middle-aged.

The Serene Sixties usually begin around retirement. For those who have built their life on busyness, activity, and accomplishments, the Sixties will not be serene but sour. These men could end their life in despair rather than with integrity and hope. You see, the paramount concern of the Sixties is: What will my life add up to? Is it too late to put more meaning in my life before I'm old? Do I want to be remembered only for this?

There's a profound recognition that there are maybe a couple of laps left around the track. How will I finish the race? This can be an incredible time of hopefulness or a time of great depression. Research shows that by this age the harbinger of emotional health in men was not a stable childhood or a high-flying career. Rather, among older men it was much more important to have developed an ability to handle life's accidents and conflicts without passivity, blaming, or bitterness.[4] Why were these men able to keep a healthy perspective? Partly because through the years they had good male friends around them. A man in this stage of life wants to make sure he leaves a solid legacy. Those who are spiritually mature will seek to empower others and be a mentor. They may retire from work but not from life.

Men who are in this stage need those around them to draw them out and make them feel needed. They need shoulder-to-shoulder brothers who will ask them to be their mentors, and assure them they do have something to offer. Men in this stage also need to be held accountable to stay involved. They need to be encouraged to keep growing and learning, as well as challenged to finish the race well (2 Tim. 4:6–7). These men need a balance of separateness and independence within a caring group.

I still have contact with one of my mentors. He's now sixty-three years old. We do not meet regularly, but we talk periodically, and he often sends me letters letting me know how valuable I am to the kingdom and sharing new insights he has learned. I want to be like him when I grow up. The Flaming Fifties and Serene Sixties are incredibly important. It's through the wisdom of men in these stages that those coming behind have hope and can maintain their perspective, passion, and purpose in life.

I've tried to share with you the key issues a man faces at the various stages of his life. There's one constant—the need for shoulder-to-shoulder brothers. No matter where we are in life, we need our brothers.

Jay Kessler is the president of Temple University. He tells a story about attending the funeral of a dear friend. He says that when he arrived and sat down, there were only a handful of people. In fact, they couldn't even find six friends to carry this man's casket. Jay said it set him wondering—if his funeral were today, would he have six friends to carry his casket? Do you have those six friends? If not, it's not too late. No matter what stage you are in, begin to seek out shoulder-to-shoulder brothers. You'll never regret it. You see, friends are like high-grade fuel—they take the knock out of living.

DISCUSSION QUESTIONS

1. Think through the stages in your life. How have they differed from what Dr. Cooper described? How are they the same? How does this chapter give you a different perspective on your life?

2. How do you view change? Have you entertained thoughts that when life got "better," it would somehow be static?

3. Dr. Cooper wrote "[The testing twenties] is a time of experimentation and exploration to determine what track he will finally end up running on to achieve his dreams." Discuss what this would mean for a man who has just come to Christ.

4. If you are not in your twenties, discuss ways to mentor those who are. What strengths do you have as a role model? What do

you think is the most important strength? If you are in your twenties, are there men in your life you look up to and respect? What is it that draws you to them?

5. Why is balance the key issue in the thirties? Read 1 Timothy 5:8. How might this verse cause men in this stage problems?

6. What are the reasons a man in the fickle forties stage has an affair? How can shoulder to shoulder brothers help someone focus on what is left and not what is lost? Read the Exodus story. What percentage of Moses' life had passed when God appeared to him and gave him a new direction?

7. Examine your church and your men's group. What is the age differential? Does your church have a good mix? Do the older people attend classes for older adults only? How is this unhealthy for the church and for your group? If you are in the fifties and sixties stage, how can you reach out to other men? If you're not in this stage yet, what steps are you taking to ensure you enter this stage successfully?

8. Reach 2 Timothy 4:5–8. Discuss the implications of this verse for each stage of a man's life.

9. Read Acts 8:1–3, 9:1–19. What stage do you think Paul was in at this time in his life? Compare this with Philippians, written later in his life. How has he changed? Discuss the changes found in Jacob (Genesis 27–33 and 48–49).

CHAPTER 11

The Blessings of Brotherhood

The nine-year-old boy had been dreading the evening for weeks. His mother insisted he attend a big-time, formal piano concert with her. She hoped it would somehow motivate him to do what he'd resisted doing for years—practice the piano every day.

The antsy kid anticipated a night with high-society snobs dressed in tuxedos and long evening dresses. He couldn't imagine anything more boring than listening to grown-ups talk about their latest vacation or art purchase. And he dreaded hearing them comment on how much he'd grown since they last saw him. Did they think maybe he should be getting shorter? Really!

He went, but not without digging in his heels. The concert hall was packed. The crowd had come to hear Ignace Jan Paderewski, the world famous composer, do his thing at the piano.

When the boy's mother turned to talk with friends, he decided to get out of his seat and get a closer look at the piano. As he approached the huge stage, which was flooded with lights, he was strangely drawn to the ebony grand Steinway and its tufted leather stool. Unnoticed by the sophisticated audience, he sat down at the stool, staring wide-eyed at the black and white keys. He placed his small, trembling fingers in the right location and began to play "Chopsticks." The roar of the crowd was hushed as thousands of frowning faces turned in his direction. Irritated and embarrassed, they began to shout:

"Get that boy away from there!"

"Who'd bring a kid like that in here?"

"Where are his parents?"

"Somebody stop him!"

Backstage the master overheard the sounds out front and quickly realized what was happening. Hurriedly he grabbed his coat and rushed toward the stage. Without a word to the crowd, he stooped over the boy, reached around both sides, and began to improvise a countermelody to harmonize with and enhance the simple song. As the two of them played together, Paderewski kept whispering in the boy's ear, "Keep going. Don't quit, son. Keep on playing.... Don't stop.... Don't quit."

The first time I read a version of that story—in *Seasons of Life*, by Chuck Swindoll—I was reminded of all the times in my life when I felt about as successful as a kid playing "Chopsticks" at a concert hall. Times when I felt that my best effort wasn't good enough. Times when I felt like giving up. On those occasions, a friend would sit down beside me and give me just the support and encouragement I needed to keep on playing, to keep going, to not give up.

I thank God for my friends. And in this final chapter, I want to share with you some of the blessings you'll experience as you develop shoulder-to-shoulder relationships with other men.

THE BLESSING

In a very real sense, I'm a blessed man. If there's one thing my dad gave me, it was a firm belief that he loved and accepted me, a conviction that he believed in me. I know from both research and experience that there's nothing a man wants and needs more than the blessing of his father. Second to that is the blessing of his friends.

The Greek word for "bless" meant "to speak well of" or "to praise someone." In Old Testament times, a blessing actually transferred a good thing from one person to another. For instance, when Isaac, under God's direction, blessed Jacob, he imparted the promise of bountiful crops, many servants, and leadership in the family (Gen. 27:27–29). Over time Jacob actually received each of those benefits.

While many of us lack the ability to give a blessing that actually transfers land, money, or influence, our words can pass on valuable gifts to our friends. Gifts like a sense of security and destiny. How can we do this?

VERBAL AFFIRMATION

Nobody illustrates the makeup of a blessing more than Jesus. Mobbed by spectators and guarded by his disciples, Jesus took the time to welcome and bless a group of little children.

Parents were bringing their kids to Jesus so he could touch them, but the disciples rebuked them. When Jesus saw this, he was indignant. He said, "Let the little children come to me, and do not hinder them, for the kingdom of heaven belongs to such as these" (Matt. 19:14). Mark 10:16 says, "And he took the children in his arms, put his hands on them and blessed them."

In the Bible, a blessing isn't a blessing until it's spoken. I remember hearing about an umpire who was being interviewed on *The Tonight Show.* Johnny Carson asked him if he ever questioned his calls afterward. The umpire said, "Johnny, some's balls and some's strikes, but they ain't nothin' till I call 'em."

The point he made was that regardless of where the ball was actually thrown, it became whatever he called it.

That's the way a blessing is. It's nothing until it's "called," or spoken.

How important is it for you to give and receive a verbal blessing? A study of maladjusted students in a large Oklahoma high school answers that question. First, the counselors in the school developed close relationships with ten of the school's most troubled teenagers. Next, the counselors asked these kids, "How long has it been since your parents told you they loved you?" Only one of the students could remember hearing it at all, and he didn't remember when.

In sharp contrast, students in the same school who were considered well-adjusted gave answers like, "This morning," "Last evening," and "Yesterday." While that research dealt with students, it makes a valid point for all ages. Namely, that words of affirmation are life-changing.

Solomon highlighted the importance of well-timed words when he wrote, "A word aptly spoken is like apples of gold in settings of silver" (Prov. 25:11). Words of affirmation uttered at the right time show the wisdom of a jeweler who places delicate golden apples in a sterling silver setting.

Our words, and those of our friends, are powerful beyond measure. Words of affirmation are one of the great blessings we receive from shoulder-to-shoulder relationships. And there's no time when they are needed more than when we're emotionally down.

WILDERNESS EXPERIENCES

The biblical friendship that demonstrates the role of affirmation best is the one between Jonathan and David. The odds against them becoming buddies were high. Jonathan was the son of King Saul. He was the heir apparent to the royal throne. David was the son of a shepherd. He was a harp player who delighted in singing songs of praise to God. Furthermore, David was the man God selected to be the next king.

In spite of the differences and potential difficulties, the men fast became friends. On the day David defeated Goliath, Jonathan saw something in David that he liked, something that told him the two would hit it off. From that time on they were best friends—they had a shoulder-to-shoulder relationship.

The text says they were "one in spirit" (1 Sam. 18:1). That doesn't mean they always thought alike. Rather, it indicates they had a sense of camaraderie. When you're one in spirit with a friend, you're truly happy when he enters a room. You share a common faith and sense of purpose.

I suspect it was their mutual zeal for God that knitted their hearts together. David had demonstrated a courageous faith in God when he took on Goliath. Jonathan had exercised a similar faith earlier when he battled the Philistines (1 Sam. 14:1–14).

To demonstrate the depth of his commitment to David, Jonathan not only made a covenant with him, he sealed the covenant by giving David his tunic, sword, bow, and belt. It's likely his sword was made of a metal that made it a unique weapon. In a very real sense, Jonathan made all he had available to David.

Following David's victory, King Saul was overcome with jealousy. In a rage, he drove David into the wilderness. Day after day, month after month, David ran from the king. Exhausted and no doubt discouraged, he hid wherever he could. On one occasion, while David was hiding in the wilderness of Ziph, Jonathan came to him. Why? The text says he "helped him find strength in God" (1 Sam. 23:16).

While David might have been able to hide from his enemy, he couldn't hide from his friend. And I don't think he wanted to. Jonathan hunted David down because he knew his friend needed his words of encouragement. He told David, "Don't be afraid. . . . My father Saul will not lay a hand on you. You will be king over Israel, and I will be second to you" (v. 17).

That statement's profound when you realize that Jonathan was in line to be the next king. He was so secure in the Lord and in his friendship with David that he gladly told his friend, "You'll be the next king." No competition. No self-protection. He saw a friend in need and blessed him with words of affirmation. Words that put his hope in God.

I recently had an experience that reminded me of the importance of my friends. I'd just recovered from a bout with pneumonia so I was physically beat. I was feeling discouraged by some ministry disappointments. I felt like hiding, but the men in my group wouldn't let me. They asked questions that slowly helped me open up. When I finally spilled my guts, one of the men said, "Rod, you know I'm busy. But I want you to know that anytime you need someone to talk with, I'll cancel everything on my schedule so we can get together." What a blessing! I'm telling you, those words were just what I needed to hear.

When I need them, my friends will always be there with the words I need to hear. The day will come when you're in the wilderness. At such times the greatest blessing in your life will be in the form of a friend, one who hunts you down and gives you the support you need to make it through the desert. And there will be times when you'll need to be a Jonathan to someone else.

PHYSICAL AFFIRMATION

It's important to note that Jesus touched the children who were brought to him. Jesus didn't just bend over and lecture the kids. He didn't sit on a stool and coolly instruct them. No! He gathered them into his arms. He hugged them. He laid his hands on their shoulders and heads. He made them feel loved.

I realize that in our society, the idea of touching is taboo for most men. But Jesus recognized the importance of physical touch. And he dramatically used his hands and arms to communicate love.

Take the case of the leper who approached Jesus. In ancient Israel, leprosy was considered the most loathsome of diseases. It was the ancient equivalent of AIDS—except everyone knew those who were infected. Lepers were outcasts. They had to wear a covering over their mouth and shout out a warning of their approach. The words "Unclean, Unclean!" caused others to move away whenever a leper came near. According to Leviticus 13–14, a leper suffered such defilement that those who touched one immediately became unclean themselves.

One day a man suffering from an advanced case of leprosy approached Jesus. Large areas of raw flesh, scabs, and white shining spots covered much of his body. An arm or leg may have already rotted off, leaving only a stub. The man probably hadn't felt the touch of a human hand or the warmth of an embrace in years, perhaps decades.

How did Jesus respond? He touched the man and then healed him. Most of us would have reversed the order of events. We would have healed the man and then touched him. But not Jesus. Mark wrote, "Filled with compassion, Jesus reached out his hand and touched the man" (Mark 1:41).

On another occasion, when Jesus saw the sick mother-in-law of Peter, "he touched her hand and the fever left her" (Matt. 8:15). In Matthew 9:29 some blind men approached Jesus and the Lord "touched their eyes." At the Mount of Transfiguration, when the disciples became terrified, "Jesus came and touched them" (Matt. 17:7).

Why did Jesus so frequently touch people? After all, he could have healed anybody with a thought or a word. He could have calmed his frightened disciples without touching them. I'm convinced that Jesus touched people because he understood the immense human need for love and acceptance.

Nothing communicates acceptance better than a hand on the shoulder, a pat on the back, or a bear hug. But most American men shy away from any kind of touching. In our society we're taught from the earliest age that touching is a feminine trait. To avoid appearing homosexual, we avoid all touching. The only exception is in the sports arena. Athletes or fans are allowed to hug, slap hands, or embrace.

Yet in other societies men frequently touch. In Mexico men greet each other with a hug. In Pakistan they hold hands. In numerous European countries they greet one another with a kiss on the cheek.

Now don't get me wrong. I'm not urging you to start greeting your friends with a kiss. Nor am I suggesting you hold hands with a friend when you walk down the street. Rather, I'm urging you to bless your friends with an occasional hug or slap on the back. During a time of anguish, nothing comforts more than a hug from a friend, an affirming and comforting touch.

To underline the importance of a touch, consider that during the nineteenth century more than half of the infants died from a disease called *maramus,* a Greek word meaning "wasting away." As late as the 1920s, the death rate for infants under one year of age in various U.S. foundling institutions was close to 100 percent. A respected New York pediatrician, Dr. Henry Chapin, observed that infants were kept in sterile, neat, tidy wards but were rarely picked up. Chapin brought in women to hold the babies, coo to them, and stroke them, and the mortality rate dropped drastically.

People need to be touched. Babies die if they're not frequently held by loving adults. Jesus understood that, so he frequently reached out and touched people who were in need. In doing so, he transformed their lives.

PREDICTIVE AFFIRMATION

Repeatedly God reminds his children of the greatness of their future. When God first spoke to Abraham, he promised to give him land, many descendants, and a special heir through whom the world would be blessed (Gen. 12:1–3). Later God promised Isaac a future to look forward to (Gen. 26:24). A generation later God appeared to Jacob in a dream and promised to give him the land upon which he slept (Gen. 28:13).

Jesus repeatedly stretched the imagination of his disciples with predictions about their future. In Matthew 19:28 he promised they would sit upon thrones, judging the twelve tribes of Israel. During the Last Supper Jesus told them he was going to prepare a dwelling place for them in his Father's house (John 14:2).

The promises haven't stopped. God also gives us wonderful pictures for the future: "When he appears, we shall be like him, for we shall see him as he is" (1 John 3:2). What a promise! One day all believers will instantly be transformed into the image of Jesus.

Fixing our hope on such a promise shapes our personalities and builds our futures. The more we imagine ourselves becoming like Jesus, the more we are like him. That's why John said, "Everyone who has this hope in him purifies himself, just as he is pure" (v. 3).

Now, we can't make predictions like those God made for Abraham, Isaac, and Jacob. We can't speak of our friend's future with the confidence John had when he spoke of a believer's destiny. But we can know our friends well enough to imagine what God might accomplish through them.

Remember what Jonathan did for David in the wilderness of Ziph. He assured him God had great plans for his life. Even though David's present seemed bleak and his future dismal, Jonathan assured David that he would one day be king. What a friend!

Such predictive affirmation is literally life-changing. A famous classroom study by Harvard psychologist Robert Rosenthal and Lenore Jacobson, a San Francisco school principal, provides a good illustration. To discover how much our expectations influence our behavior, they administered a series of learning and aptitude tests to a group of kindergarten through fifth-grade students. The results of the tests were tabulated, and at the start of the next school year, the researchers casually gave teachers the names of five or six students who had been identified as fast learners.

What the teachers didn't know was that the names of the students had been chosen at random. Those identified were simply a cross section of the student body. At the end of the year, all the children were tested again, with some astonishing results. The pupils whom the teachers had thought possessed the most potential actually scored far better and had gained as many as fifteen to twenty-seven IQ points. The teachers described these children as happier, more curious, and more affectionate than the average student. They described them as having a better chance of success later in life.[1]

The only change that had initially occurred was in the minds of the teachers. They believed in these kids and communicated their faith in them. The result? Changed lives. Improved performance. The power of predictive affirmation is profound.

One of the greatest blessings of brotherhood is developing friendships with men whose faith in God and in you is such that they look for the best. They anticipate that God will accomplish something good in and through your life. Like Jonathan, they can see and expect the best even when times are darkest.

I mentioned earlier that I was recently discouraged and the men in my group offered me words of support. I didn't tell you the whole story. I was so down, I questioned if I'd ever accomplish anything in the ministry. Man, I was really discouraged. One of the men looked at me with tears in his eyes and said, "Rod, I believe God is going to use you greatly. There are books you'll write and sermons you'll preach. God is going to use you in a mighty way. And during those times when you can't believe that, call me on the phone and I'll believe for you."

"I KNEW YOU'D COME"

I'll never forget reading the story of a marine who was caught in an ambush by the Viet Cong. Somehow he managed to find safety in a hole. But his best friend was cut down by sniper fire out in the open. As the marine kept his head down, he heard the cries of his buddy calling out to him for help. "John, I'm hit. I think it's bad. I can't see."

After several grueling minutes, John told his commanding officer he was going to crawl out and retrieve his buddy. "It's a waste of time," his superior said. "He's hit too bad. He'll die no matter what you do."

"I want to go anyway. He's my buddy."

"Go ahead," his commanding officer said. "But you'll probably both end up dead."

While the rest of his squad provided cover, John crawled to his buddy's side. What he found was worse then he'd imagined. "I'm here," he said.

His friend opened his eyes and smiled. Collecting his final bit of strength, he said, "I knew you'd come." Having uttered those words, he died.

John managed to make it back to the squad. "He was alive when I got there," John said. "But he was hit bad and died while I was at his side."

"I told you that you were wasting your time," his superior said.

"No, I wasn't," John replied. "Just before he died, he looked at me and said, 'I knew you'd come.' He died knowing I was there for him."

I don't know if that story is true or not. But I do know it illustrates the love and blessing men can give to each other, the love and blessing that I hope you'll have the courage and faith to discover. If you do, you'll find that standing shoulder to shoulder with your friends is the best way to stand tall and strong during the good times and the bad. You'll find it's the surest way to become the man you want to be. And the man God wants to make of you.

DISCUSSION QUESTIONS

1. Have you ever had the experience of being blessed? When? How did it make you feel? If you haven't, what would it mean to you? Who would you most want to be blessed by?
2. Dr. Cooper said, "In the Bible, a blessing isn't a blessing until it's spoken." Discuss how this might apply to Christ being the "word of God."
3. Is it possible to verbally bless yourself?
4. Everyone has heard a man say at one time or another, "I don't need to tell her I love her, she knows it." According to this chapter, why isn't that good enough? Can you make a commitment to begin verbally blessing those around you, including your family and friends? If not, what steps do you need to take to get there?
5. When you are in the wilderness someone is in a wilderness? Read Matthew 4:1–11. What conclusion can you draw from the conclusion of Jesus' wilderness experience?

6. How comfortable are you with touch? What does Jesus heal when he touches? Do all of his miracles involve touch? Why or why not? Look back on your life. What part has touch played?

7. Why do sports offer an exception to the "no touch" message? Do sports offer exceptions to other societal messages or rules?

8. Read Jesus' predictive blessing of Peter in Matthew 16:13–20. What impact do you imagine that had on Peter? What is the predictive element in changing someone's name? Discuss Revelation 2:17. How can you bless your friends in this way?

9. Read Matthew 28:20, John 14:27–28. Why was it so important for Jesus to let us know that he would not leave us? In the movie *City Slickers,* Mitch leaves his friends and then comes back. Discuss his transformation as well as that of his friends.

10. What kind of man does God want to make you?

Notes

Part 1 — The Isolated Man

1. Hiding

    1. Larry Crabb, *The Silence of Adam* (Grand Rapids: Zondervan, 1995), 104, emphasis added.
    2. Source unknown.

2. Addiction

    1. Gerald G. May, *Addiction and Grace* (San Francisco: Harper & Row, 1988), 24–25.
    2. Lawrence J. Hatterer, *The Plesaure Addicts* (New York: A. S. Barnes, 1980), 17.
    3. Craig Nakken, *The Addictive Personality* (New York: Harper & Row, 1988), 5.
    4. Bill Perkins, *Fatal Attractions* (Eugene, Ore.: Harvest House, 1991), 26.
    5. Abraham Twersky, *Addictive Thinking* (San Francisco: Harper & Row, 1990), 61.
    6. Eugene H. Peterson, *The Message* (Colorado Springs: NavPress, 1993), 41.
    7. Erich Fromm, *Sane Society* (New York: Fawcett, 1977).

3. Stress

    1. Richard E. Ecker, *The Stress Myth* (Downers Grove, Ill.: InterVarsity Press), 20–21.

2. Robert M. Sapolsky, *Why Zebras Don't Have Ulcers* (New York: W. H. Freeman), 15–16.

3. Georgia Witkin, *The Male Stress Syndrome* (New York: New Market, 1994), 36.

4. Ibid., 38–39.

5. Ibid., 46.

6. Ibid., 48.

7. Sapolsky, *Why Zebras Don't Have Ulcers,* 111–12.

8. Witkin, *The Male Stress Syndrome,* 30–31.

9. Marvin Allen, *Angry Men, Passive Men* (New York: Ballantine, 1993), 13.

10. Eugene H. Peterson, *The Message* (Colorado Springs: NavPress, 1993), 26.

4. Meaninglessness

1. Harold Kushner, *When All You've Ever Wanted Isn't Enough* (New York: Simon & Schuster, 1987), 42–43.

2. Herb Goldberg, *The Hazards of Being a Male* (New York: Signet, 1976), 114.

Part 2 – Moving toward Brotherhood

5. Facing Reality

1. Larry Kreider, *Bottom Line Faith* (Wheaton, Ill.: Tyndale, 1996), 10.

2. "Be Thou My Vision," *The New Church Hymnal* (Lexicon Music, 1976), 8.

6. In Process

1. Plan adapted from Robert Hemfelt et al., *The Path to Serenity* (Nashville: Nelson, 1991), 88–115.

Part 3 — Strategies for Achieving Brotherhood

8. Breaking Through Relational Barriers

1. Adapted from Alan Loy McGinnis, *The Friendship Factor* (Minneapolis: Augsburg, 1979), 40–41.

2. Jack Cranfield and Mark Victor Hansen, *Chicken Soup for the Soul* (Deerfield Beach, Fl.: Health Communications, 1993), 25.

9. What Works for You

Good books for further information:

William Moulton Martson, *Emotions of Normal People* (Minneapolis: Persona Press, 1979).

Ken Voges and Ron Braund, *Understanding How Others Misunderstand You* (Chicago: Moody Press, 1990).

10. Accountability and the Stages of Man's Life

1. Daniel J. Levinson, *The Seasons of a Man's Life* (New York: Ballantine, 1978), 60.

2. Gail Sheehy, *New Passages: Mapping Your Life across Time* (New York: Ballantine, 1995), 276.

3. Ibid., 265.

4. Ibid., 356.

11. The Blessings of Brotherhood

1. Alan Loy McGinnis, *Bringing Out the Best in People* (Minneapolis: Augsburg: 1985), 33.

Double Bind

Rodney L. Cooper, Ph.D

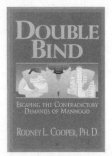

ESCAPING THE CONTRADICTORY
DEMANDS OF MANHOOD

RODNEY L. COOPER, PH.D.

If You're Like Most Men, cultural demands have turned you into an emotional chameleon. You're expected to be aggressive at work, yet nurturing at home; guarded in public but sensitive in private.

Dr. Rodney Cooper calls such contradictory demands "double binds"—no win situations men face every day, such as:

The Identity Double Bind — A man's identity is reduced to the roles he plays rather than who he really is—but he can't adequately fulfill his roles without a firm sense of his true identity.

The Breadwinner Double Bind — The man who provides for his family hears complaints that his job keeps him from giving more of himself to his wife and children.

The Companionship Double Bind — The husband who spends all his spare time with his wife, as society expects, forfeits the benefits of friendships with other men.

Men caught in double binds expend their energy trying to be everything to everyone. Consequently, they never dig deep into the heart of masculinity to discover for themselves their true identity and the freedom it brings.

Fortunately, there's a way to break free from the double binds in your life. Drawing on Dr. Cooper's experience as a professional counselor to men, *Double Bind* first explores the most prevalent double binds men face today, and points to a proven path for resolving each one. Then it unfolds biblical principles for living the Abundant Life: a life characterized by peace and assurance, grounded on a clear understanding of who you are and Whose you are.

If you're feeling squeezed and torn from opposite directions, consult *Double Bind* for a way off of the rack.... and onto the pathway of freedom, purpose, and manhood the way God designed it. Pick up your copy at local Christian bookstores today!

Double Bind 0-310-20324-4 Hardcover
Also available on audio cassette 0-310-20489-5

ZondervanPublishingHouse
Grand Rapids, Michigan
http://www.zondervan.com

A Division of HarperCollins*Publishers*